The
More Than Chicken
Cookbook

The More Than Chicken Cookbook

Sara Pitzer

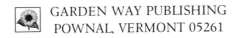 GARDEN WAY PUBLISHING
POWNAL, VERMONT 05261

Illustrations by Elayne Sears

Printed in the United States

Printing (last digit): 10 9 8 7 6 5 4 3 2 1

Library of Congress Cataloging in Publication Data

Pitzer, Sara.
  The more than chicken cookbook.

  Includes index.
  1. Cookery (Poultry) I. Title.
TX750.P58 1984   641.6'65   83–48975
ISBN 0-88266-368-2

Contents

For Sara Dietrick, Edith Pennington, and Dorothy Dietrick.
They taught me about good food.
And for Lee and Dana, who are learning about it
much faster than I did.

PREFACE

A few generations ago, poultry was special food. My grand-mother's diary, written in what seems to have been a simpler time, before supermarkets and deep-freezes, describes Sunday dinner, "Preacher and Mrs. came for dinner. Chicken and dumplings. Mrs. asked for my recipe."

Some time later, President Franklin Roosevelt promised a chicken in every pot. And the closer we came to have it, the less we appreciated it. By the 1950s many people considered poultry pedestrian because it was so readily available.

Now we have come full circle. Today's emphasis on eating less red meat, the relatively high cost of *all* food, the new trend of raising game birds domestically for market, and the wonderful experiments of many greater and lesser gourmet cooks have returned poultry to the forefront of good eating, where our ancestors always knew it belonged.

Although I intend this to be a modern cookbook, I hope the influence of our ancestors shows through. I hope you will catch glimpses of their willingness to experiment with whatever birds were available—from chickens to pigeons. I hope you will share their understanding that there is no one right way to cook poultry, or anything else for that matter. I hope you will indulge in their uninhibited enjoyment of good food well cooked. And, as you experiment with recipes using chicken parts or leftover turkey or an unfamiliar game bird, I hope you will allow yourself flights of fancy as you imagine how such concepts worked themselves into our cooking, how a little leftover turkey one day got combined with a bit of extra gravy and a handful of noodles to become potpie. Or how someone noticed that breasts were special enough to demand company treatment. Or how someone with a regard for life understood that any bird that was killed deserved respectful treatment in the kitchen.

If you cook just to eat, you can make do with a box of cornflakes and a can of mushroom soup. If you cook because eating is part of life and because it links us with lives before our own, you can experiment endlessly with the pleasure of combining the wisdom of very old cookbooks with the conveniences of today's kitchen, farm, and grocery store.

That is what I have tried to do here; and where the influence of a particular person or old recipe or folkway has been especially strong in my creating a recipe, I have noted it so you can share my sense of pulling the past into the future—and eating fantastically well in the process.

A WORD ABOUT THE RECIPES

If you've ever had chicken roasted on a spit or grilled over charcoal, you know you can cook a delicious bird with no special equipment at all. But some of today's appliances produce outstanding results with poultry, and so I have marked those recipes I find especially suited to the slow cooker, clay pot, blender, or food processor. Although every recipe in this book can be made without special equipment, I find those I've marked turn out especially well or more easily with the help of the indicated appliance. This is especially true of those recipes suggesting you use the kind of porous clay pot you soak in water first. These produce such perfectly cooked poultry, so easily, it seems anyone who expects to cook poultry more than once a month would do well to buy a clay pot or two.

But I firmly believe that the cook, not the equipment, makes a good meal, so if you like the sound of a recipe and don't have the recommended appliance, try the recipe anyway, using my alternate directions. No recipe should ever be lost for want of a gadget!

By and large, this is a "start from scratch" cookbook, using fresh ingredients and avoiding processed foods. A couple of exceptions merit note and explanation. First, canned and fresh cooked tomatoes are used interchangeably, especially in stew-type recipes. When your garden is full of tomatoes, use those; in the middle of winter, go to your shelf of Mason jars or even to the canned vegetable section of the grocery store. A second exception is that some recipes call for cooked *or canned* dried beans. Those beans you buy dried and cook yourself are much cheaper and taste a little better; but in a pinch I have found the grocery store cans of unseasoned white, pinto, and kidney beans quite acceptable—and quick. Their flavor improves if you drain and rinse them before proceeding with the recipe.

If your ear for consistency hears a certain casualness in my references to using or ignoring appliances, interchanging canned and fresh tomatoes, and substituting canned for home-cooked dried beans, you hear right. Poultry lends itself to casual cooking. It adapts to all kinds of seasonings, blends with a tremendous number of other ingredients, and cooks well by almost any method. You have to calculate fractions to make good quick breads. Soufflés require attention to detail. But you have to work pretty hard to spoil poultry. Some of the best recipes in this book resulted from "mistakes" I made trying to cook something else. If I originally intended to use half a cup of red wine in an invention and then found I had none, I may have substituted white wine for wine vinegar, or even water, and liked the results well enough to use the recipe as altered by necessity.

I'm making a big thing of the casual approach because that's how I want you to use the recipes in this cookbook. If a recipe calls for two cups of tomatoes and you have only one cup of tomato juice, don't worry about it. Adjust. Compensate. You may come up with something better than my invention.

This approach leads us to considering salt. Nobody knows what to do about salt these days. We keep hearing that it's bad for us and at the same time we're trying to cook for people who don't care, they want to use it anyhow. The solution, in this cookbook, is the phrase "salt to taste," in all except those recipes where I find a particular amount necessary for it to taste right. My first plan was to indicate each recipe I thought could be prepared successfully without any salt at all, but as I went along, I realized most of them could. I switched my tactic to indicating those recipes which I thought definitely *needed* salt to taste right. You'll notice there aren't many of them. The rest say "salt to taste," and it's up to you to decide how much to add or whether to skip it entirely.

In cooking at home, I rarely use salt, and I've noticed that few people add any at the table. When you are cooking with tasty, fresh ingredients and have herbs and spices and wine and lemon juice as flavorings, salt becomes irrelevant. I suspect we've fallen into the habit of using too much salt in an attempt to make the tasteless, overprocessed, styrofoam-and-cardboard convenience foods have any taste at all. If yours is a family that uses too much salt, try gradually reducing the amount you use in cooking, starting with these recipes. Your family may surprise you with how easily they cut down.

Finally, you will see that many recipes in this book carry the notation "1 to 100" underneath the title. That's because, in my life, at least, the number of people around to eat any given meal fluctuates more than the stock market (no pun intended). Since I can never see a potential diner go unfed, and since I like to eat well even when I am alone, I have devised the "1 to 100" recipes to cover all eventualities. Well, almost all eventualities. I really do draw the line at 101 guests.

My family and friends (and occasionally even strangers) have consumed much poultry while I created this cookbook. As you begin experimenting with poultry, too, I wish you as many good guests and as much good eating as I have enjoyed.

Some Tips
On Cooking Poultry

Believe me, there's nothing complicated about cooking poultry. I've just gathered together a few tips here for those of you who would like to shop more efficiently and handle poultry more confidently in the kitchen.

STORING AND FREEZING POULTRY

Fresh poultry can be stored in the refrigerator safely for two days. If it came in a specially sealed and dated package from the grocery store, leave it in that package; if wrapped otherwise, rewrap in aluminum foil.

Cooked poultry will keep for about a week in the refrigerator.

In the freezer, poultry can be kept for up to two months if the freezer is part of your refrigerator; it will keep for about six months in a freezer that maintains a constant temperature of 0°F. For freezing, the poultry should be wrapped in freezer-weight foil or plastic and sealed securely with all the air forced out. If you are freezing poultry you have butchered yourself, it is imperative to chill the poultry thoroughly before freezing. Otherwise, the thawed bird will smell awful and will not be safe to eat.

Cooked poultry will keep for two to three weeks in the freezer if wrapped airtight. One of the best ways to freeze cooked poultry is with some gravy or broth around it—all well chilled before going into the freezer.

It is better to thaw frozen poultry slowly in the refrigerator than on the counter of a warm kitchen. And once poultry has been defrosted, never refreeze it. Much has been made of using a microwave oven for defrosting poultry in a hurry. At best, it works only moderately well, and the meat is never as good as it is when thawed more slowly. If you decide to try it, in an emergency, use the instructions and heat setting specified for your particular brand and model oven. Generally, you set the microwave at a low or medium-low temperature and microwave the frozen poultry for about ten minutes a pound. Usually you have to turn the bird several times to insure that it thaws evenly. And if the bird has been frozen with any metal in it, a wire truss for the legs, for instance, you can't put it in the microwave oven at all, unless you can pry the wire from the frozen meat. It seems to me that when you need to cook something in a hurry, it is easier to fix something else and save your frozen poultry for when you have time to attend to it properly.

The one place a microwave can be useful is where you need a small amount of cooked poultry to use in a recipe. Then you can thaw a couple of breasts or a leg or quarter and cook it in the microwave oven in a few minutes, following the temperature settings and times recommended by your owners' manual.

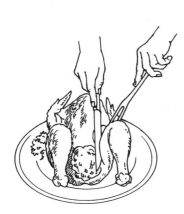

Holding the drumstick, run the knife between the thigh and the body.

CARVING POULTRY

A heavy, sharp knife and a cavalier attitude toward carving will get you through the task like a pro. Carve on a large serving platter that does not have delicate edges, or on a cutting board. Boards and platters with wells or troughs to catch the juice and keep it from running onto the table are nice.

Let the bird stand for fifteen to thirty minutes before carving, depending on its size.

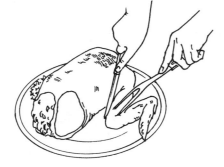

Cut above the wing joint into the body.

1. Take hold of a drumstick and pull it away from the body. Run the knife between the thigh and the body of the bird and cut down to the joint. Pull the leg off the body, using the point of the knife at the

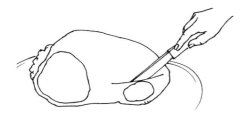

Cut into the breast meat at the wing joint.

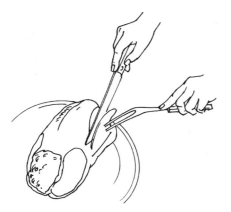

Slice breast meat.

joint to help get it loose. Cut the thigh and the drumstick at the joint on larger birds.

2. Stick a fork into the upper wing to hold the bird and cut above the wing joint into the body. Remove the wing. Cut into the breast meat, from the skin into the bone at the wing joint.

3. Slice breast meat straight down from the outer edges of the breast, making one slice after another. Each slice will fall free when your knife reaches the cut above the wing bone. Keep slicing the white meat, starting each cut at a higher point on the breast.

4. If the thigh and drumstick are very large, slice meat from them.

Repeat the process on the other side of the bird.

MAKING STOCK

The miracle is that anybody makes stock at all these days, given the dreadfully complicated instructions for doing it that abound. We must have persisted because poultry stock is so useful to have around, not only for soups, but also for stews and sauces and as the flavoring agent for all sorts of concoctions.

And it's no big deal. If you'll just put whatever bones and skin you have from your poultry into a pan, cover them with water, put the lid on, bring to a boil, and simmer for a couple of hours, you'll have stock. I prefer simmering raw bones and leftover skeletons separately, but you don't have to; the resulting stock is just a little more cloudy when you mix them. Sometimes I add a little celery and onion for extra flavor, and maybe an eggshell or two for a dab of calcium, but you don't have to bother with that either, unless you want to.

To make your stock extra strong or concentrated, continue to simmer the stock until it has reduced somewhat.

If your stock is fatty, refrigerate for several hours. Then skim off the fat that rises to the surface and congeals.

If you do go in for heavy-duty stock making, with the extra vegetables and eggshells, try to do it in private moments to save yourself the embarrassment I suffered when my teenage daughter's boyfriend first saw my stock pot. He'd been prowling in the kitchen, lifting the lid on this and that, and eventually got to the stock kettle. He saw the onion peels and celery leaves and eggshells simmering away with turkey bones. I thought he put the lid down rather hastily. A moment later, I heard him asking my daughter, "How come your mom boils the garbage?"

SAFETY REMINDER

Perhaps you remember your grandmother stuffing the turkey the night before a big meal so that she would have a head start on the preparations next day. Today food scientists warn us that the practice is dangerous. The conditions inside that bird encourage the growth of deadly salmonella bacteria if the dressing is allowed to stand uncooked there. It is better to prepare the dressing and refrigerate it separately, stuffing the bird just before roasting.

If your turkey weighs more than twenty pounds, bake the dressing separately. According to food scientists, heat penetrates too slowly at weights higher than twenty pounds, again creating conditions hospitable to the growth of dangerous bacteria.

Finally, when the meal is done, remove all stuffing from the cavity of the cooked poultry. Refrigerate the leftover stuffing separately, and remove the meat from the bones of the cooked bird before refrigerating.

These practices differ from the old-fashioned ways many of us first learned; and though they may seem less romantic, they are much safer.

QUICK TIPS

• Save the fat you pull loose from chickens, fry it out gently over medium heat in a heavy skillet, and pour into a small container. Covered in the refrigerator, it will stay good for about a week and is nice as a flavored cooking fat. However, don't use it for sautés; chicken fat spatters excessively on high heat. Cook with chicken fat over medium or low heat.

• When a recipe calls for cooked poultry, you can use chicken, turkey, or other birds' meat interchangeably.

• When buying "fresh" turkey parts, be sure they are not actually frozen parts that have been thawed and put into the fresh meat case for the convenience of shoppers. The label must be explicit.

• When cooked poultry seems too dry to use, shred it and simmer it in barbecue sauce for "sloppy Jims."

• Herbs especially good with chicken and turkey are tarragon, thyme, parsley, chervil, chives, sage, and bay leaf.

• Herbs especially good with Cornish hens, ducks, and geese are juniper berries, marjoram, sage, rosemary, and thyme.

• Frozen cooked poultry keeps better if you add a small quantity of gravy to the package before freezing it.

Chicken and Turkey Appetizers

Chicken Packages

TIME: 2 HOURS MARINATING;
  15 MINUTES BAKING
YIELD: 12 PACKAGES

Based on a Chinese cooking technique, this recipe is some bother, but fun. The Chinese would fry the foil-wrapped packages in deep fat, but baking them in the oven is easier and safer. If you don't have Chinese five spice powder, substitute pinches of cinnamon and clove. If you don't have hoisin sauce, substitute apple butter. Both ingredients are available wherever Chinese foods are sold.

6 chicken drumsticks
1 tablespoon pineapple juice
1 teaspoon hoisin sauce
  (or apple butter)
1 teaspoon sherry
¼ teaspoon grated fresh ginger
  root
⅛ teaspoon five spice powder
¼ teaspoon salt
1½ tablespoons cornstarch

Remove the meaty part from each drumstick and cut into two pieces. (Save the bones for stock.) Combine the pineapple juice, hoisin sauce, sherry, ginger, five spice powder, salt, and cornstarch. Marinate the chicken pieces in the mixture, refrigerated, for about 2 hours.

Preheat the oven to 375°F.

Cut 12 squares of heavy-duty aluminum foil, each measuring about 8 inches. Place a piece of marinated chicken on each square and fold a corner over the chicken. Roll the foil toward the opposite corner 2 or 3 times, then fold in the side corners. Finally, wrap the last corner around the roll, squeezing the foil firmly against the chicken. Bake the packages on a cookie sheet for about 15 minutes, until the chicken is juicy and tender. (If you want to try the frying technique, deep fry in hot oil for about 5 minutes.)

Serve the chicken hot, in the packages.

Chicken Liver Pâté With Mock Truffles

TIME: ABOUT 30 MINUTES
   COOKING; AT LEAST 3 HOURS
   CHILLING
YIELD: ABOUT 3½ CUPS
FOOD PROCESSOR

This recipe was a gift. I had been collecting paté recipes for over a year and was still looking for what I considered a "just right" chicken liver paté, when I got a Christmas card from a friend with this recipe, clipped from heaven-knows-where included. Originally the recipe called for a cup of finely chopped parsley as a garnish, but I didn't like the tast combination. Somehow, in fooling around with variations, I hit upon the walnuts, which produce a texture much like that of truffles in paté. It is excellent served with sweet onion slices.

2 pounds chicken livers
2 tablespoons butter
½ cup chopped onion
¼ cup strong chicken stock
3-ounce package cream cheese
½ cup butter at room temperature
½ teaspoon powdered thyme
¼ teaspoon pepper
salt to taste
¼ cup finely chopped nuts
   (preferably black walnuts)

Rinse and drain the livers. Let them dry slightly on paper towels. Melt 2 tablespoons butter in a heavy skillet, add the livers and onion, and sauté until the livers are just cooked through, about 2 minutes. Finely chop the mixture with a knife on a flat cutting board, or puree it in a food processor.

If you are using a food processor, blend in the stock, cream cheese, ½ cup butter, and seasonings, dropping them through the feed tube a little at a time. If you are mixing by hand, put the liver and onions in a bowl and gradually work in the other ingredients with a fork or wooden spoon. Either way, continue mixing until everything is well blended and smooth. Finally, work in the nuts so they are just incorporated but not turned to mush.

Pack the pâté into a small crock or shape into a ball and refrigerate for at least 3 hours before serving.

Chicken Liver Pâté With Bacon

TIME: 30 MINUTES PREPARING;
  30 MINUTES CHILLING
YIELD: 4–6 SERVINGS
FOOD PROCESSOR

1 quart water
1 pound chicken livers
12 slices bacon
4 hard-boiled eggs
½ cup mayonnaise (page 110)
1 medium-size sweet onion,
  chopped
salt to taste

Another variation on an old classic. The bacon here adds a completely different character to the pâté. Use it as a spread or serve on lettuce.

Bring the water to a boil and drop the livers, a few at a time, into the water. Simmer gently for 10–15 minutes, until they are just done through. Drain and cool.

Fry the bacon until crisp and crumble it into a large bowl.

With the food processor or by hand, chop the livers and add them to the bacon. Chop the eggs and add them to the livers. Stir in the mayonnaise, adding more or less to get a consistency you like. Stir in the onion. Salt to taste and chill for at least 30 minutes before serving.

Cold Chicken Livers

TIME: 10 MINUTES COOKING;
  2 HOURS CHILLING
YIELD: 4–6 SERVINGS

1 pound chicken livers
1 cup stock
3 tablespoons chopped fresh
  parsley (do not substitute dried)
2 tablespoons red wine vinegar
pinch cinnamon
pinch ginger
salt to taste

Simmer the livers in the stock for 5–10 minutes, until they are just tender and no longer pink. Do not overcook. Drain and chill. Before serving, mix the parsley, vinegar, spices, and a little salt. Pour this mixture over the livers. Chill for at least 2 hours and serve cold.

Chopped Chicken Livers

TIME: 30 MINUTES PREPARING;
   30 MINUTES CHILLING
YIELD: 1½ CUPS
FOOD PROCESSOR

1 quart water
1 pound chicken livers
4 hard-boiled eggs
1 medium-size sweet onion
¼ cup mayonnaise (page 110)
½ teaspoon pepper
salt to taste

Traditional Jewish recipes for chopped chicken liver use chicken fat as the moistening ingredient. This version, using mayonnaise, probably is better for you. It tastes almost the same and keeps longer in the refrigerator.

Bring the water to a boil and drop in the chicken livers, a few at a time. Simmer gently for about 15 minutes or until the livers are just cooked through. Do not overcook. Drain and cool the livers, then chill for at least 30 minutes. Peel and chill the eggs. Finely chop the livers, eggs, and onion. If you use a food processor, cut the eggs and onions into big chunks and put them into the mixing bowl with the livers, mayonnaise, and seasonings, and process in short spurts, being careful not to overprocess and produce baby food. If you use a knife and cutting board, it will be easier to chop each ingredient separately, scraping them into a mixing bowl as you go. After all ingredients are chopped, work in the mayonnaise and seasonings.

Serve as an appetizer, on lettuce leaves, or as a sandwich filling.

Italian Wings

TIME: 24 HOURS MARINATING;
  40 MINUTES BAKING
YIELD: 6 SERVINGS

12 chicken wings
juice of 1 lemon
juice of 1 lime
1 garlic clove, minced
3 tablespoons chopped fresh
  parsley
2 teaspoons chopped fresh oregano
  or 1 teaspoon dried
2 teaspoons chopped fresh
  tarragon or 1 teaspoon dried
½ cup olive oil
2-3 cups dried bread crumbs
1 teaspoon dried oregano
salt to taste

Place the wings in a bowl. Combine the lemon and lime juices, garlic, parsley, oregano, tarragon, and olive oil. Pour over the wings. Marinate overnight.

About 1 hour before you want to serve, preheat the oven to 375°F. Remove the chicken from the marinade. Combine the bread crumbs, dried oregano, and salt. Roll the wings in the crumb mixture and arrange them in a flat baking dish so they do not touch each other. Cover the dish with foil and bake for 25 minutes. Remove the foil and continue baking about 15 minutes more, or until brown.

These wings are delicious served hot, warm, or at room temperature.

Barbecued Wings

TIME: 1 HOUR
YIELD: 6 SERVINGS

12 chicken wings
1 cup tomato sauce
3 tablespoons brown sugar
1 tablespoon soy sauce

Preheat the oven to 400°F. Arrange the wings in a flat baking pan so they do not touch each other and bake for 30 minutes. While the wings are baking, cook the tomato sauce, sugar, and soy sauce together until the sugar has dissolved. When the 30 minutes baking time is up, thickly spread the sauce over the wings and return the wings to the oven to bake for 30–40 minutes more, or until they are nicely browned and very tender. You can brush the wings with sauce once or twice more, but it really is not necessary. Serve warm.

Chinese Chicken Wings

TIME: 1 HOUR MARINATING;
    40–50 MINUTES BAKING
YIELD: 6 SERVINGS

1 garlic clove, minced
1 cup soy sauce
12 chicken wings

You'll like these wings for appetizers, snacks, lunches, buffets, and picnics.

Combine the garlic and soy sauce. Add the chicken wings and marinate for 1–6 hours in the refrigerator.
   Preheat the oven to 400°F.
   Arrange the marinated wings on a cookie sheet or flat pan so they do not touch each other. You can save the remaining marinade to use again if you keep it refrigerated. Bake the chicken for 40–50 minutes, turning once or twice to be sure the wings brown evenly. Serve hot or cold.

Sesame Wings

TIME: 40 MINUTES
YIELD: 6 SERVINGS
BLENDER

1 cup sesame seeds
2 tablespoons flour
2 teaspoons seasoning salt
2 eggs
1 tablespoon oil
12 chicken wings

Preheat the oven to 400°F. Grind about half the sesame seeds in a blender. If you don't have a blender, leave all the seeds whole and roll them on a board with a rolling pin to crush slightly. Mix the whole and ground seeds in a bowl with the flour and seasoning salt.

Beat the eggs with the oil in a separate bowl. Dip the wings first into the egg mixture, then into the seed mixture. Arrange the wings on an oiled cookie sheet or flat pan so they do not touch each other. Bake for 40 minutes, or until the outsides of the wings are crisp and brown. Good hot or cold.

Chicken or Turkey Spread

TIME: 15 MINUTES PREPARING;
   1–2 HOURS CHILLING
YIELD: 1 CUP
FOOD PROCESSOR
GOOD USE OF LEFTOVERS

1 cup (cold) cooked chicken or
   turkey
3 tablespoons mayonnaise
   (page 110)
1 tablespoon prepared mustard
1 slice raw onion
salt to taste

Try this spread as an appetizer, served in little mounds on lettuce leaves as you would chopped liver. Of course, it makes a wonderful sandwich, too.

If you are preparing this spread in the food processor, put the chicken or turkey into the mixing bowl in medium-size chunks, and process in short spurts until the poultry is *coarsely* ground. Add the mayonnaise, mustard, onion, and salt. Process until all the ingredients are just mixed together. Do not overprocess. To prepare without a food processor, chop the poultry and onion with a knife and then work in the other ingredients with a fork. Chill for 1–2 hours before serving.

Chicken and Turkey Soups

Chicken Noodle and Bean Soup

TIME: 30 MINUTES, AFTER STOCK
  IS PREPARED AND BEANS ARE
  COOKED
YIELD: 8 SERVINGS
GOOD USE OF LEFTOVER CHICKEN

People remember this soup. I think it is absolutely first class, good enough for a dinner party and easy enough for everyday lunch. You can store it in the refrigerator for several days. The combination of beans, pasta, and chicken provides a lot of protein value for the relatively small amount of chicken you use and makes the soup more satisfying than most chicken soups.

1 tablespoon butter or rendered
  chicken fat
1 celery rib, chopped
1 small onion, chopped
1 carrot, chopped
6 cups chicken stock
2 cups fine dry noodles
1 cup chopped cooked chicken
½ cup chopped canned tomatoes
  or peeled and chopped fresh
  tomatoes
1 cup cooked white beans with
  their liquid (canned beans are
  acceptable here)
½ cup dry white wine
salt and pepper to taste
chopped fresh parsley

Melt the butter in a soup kettle over medium heat. Add the celery, onion, and carrot, and sauté until they begin to soften. Do not brown. Add the chicken stock and bring to a boil over high heat. Stir in the noodles and bring back to a boil as quickly as possible. Add the remaining ingredients, except for the parsley and seasonings. Reduce the heat slightly and continue cooking until the noodles are done, about 10–15 minutes. Add salt and pepper to taste. This is one recipe which really does seem to need a little salt to pull all the flavors together. Garnish each serving with a sprinkling of parsley.

Chicken Gumbo

TIME: 40 MINUTES
YIELD: 6 SERVINGS
GOOD USE OF LEFTOVER CHICKEN

Simply delicious!

2 slices bacon, diced
1 large onion, chopped
½ green pepper, chopped
1½ cups fresh or frozen okra, cut
  in ½-inch circles
1 celery rib, chopped
2 cups canned or cooked tomatoes
1½ cups chicken stock
1½ cups chopped cooked chicken
½ bay leaf
¼ teaspoon hot pepper sauce
½ teaspoon fresh thyme or
  ¼ teaspoon dried
salt to taste

Fry the bacon until crisp in a soup kettle. Pour off all but about 1 tablespoon of the fat. Keeping the heat high, rapidly sauté the onion pepper, okra, and celery, stirring constantly. Stop as soon as the ingredients begin to soften. The importance of this step is that the quick, high heat seals the okra so that it doesn't make long, gelatinous strings in the soup. Add the tomatoes, stock, chicken and seasonings to the kettle. Bring just to a boil, and simmer gently for 20–30 minutes, or until the okra is just tender. Do not overcook.

For a hearty meal, serve over rice. Allow about ½ cup cooked rice per serving.

Velvet Corn Soup

TIME: 10 MINUTES
YIELD: 6 SERVINGS

Even if you ordinarily don't buy canned corn, it's worth keeping a can around to make this soup when you need something elegant in a hurry. The recipe is Chinese in origin, though there's not a bean sprout in sight.

3 cups chicken stock
8¾-ounce can cream-style corn
  (1–1½ cups)
1 tablespoon cornstarch
2 tablespoons cold water
2 egg whites (optional)

Bring the stock to a boil in a soup kettle. Add the corn. Soften the cornstarch in the cold water and stir into the soup. Allow to simmer, stirring occasionally, for about 5 minutes, or until the soup has thickened slightly and lost the cloudiness caused by the cornstarch. Beat the egg whites with a fork until frothy and stir them into the soup. Serve at once.

Chicken Noodle Soup

TIME: 20 MINUTES
YIELD: 8 SERVINGS
GOOD USE OF LEFTOVERS

Substitute turkey for chicken if that's what you have around.

1 tablespoon butter
1 small onion, chopped
1 celery rib, chopped
2 mushrooms, sliced
2 cups diced cooked chicken or
  turkey
¼ teaspoon dried thyme
½ small bay leaf
¼ teaspoon pepper
salt to taste
4 cups chicken or turkey stock
4 ounces dry noodles
1 cup fresh or frozen green peas

Melt the butter in a soup kettle and sauté in it the onion, celery, and mushrooms. Add the poultry and seasonings. Pour in the stock and bring to a boil. Add the dry noodles, a few at a time, and return to a boil. Continue cooking for 10–15 minutes, or until the noodles are tender. Stir in the peas and cook just long enough to soften them, no more than 5 minutes, for they should not be mushy. Serve at once.

Easy Chicken Rice Soup

TIME: 10 MINUTES
YIELD: 6 SERVINGS
GOOD USE OF LEFTOVER CHICKEN

3 cups chicken stock
1 cup diced cooked chicken
2 cups cooked rice
1 celery rib, chopped
1 small onion, minced
1 tablespoon chopped fresh parsley
salt to taste

Here's proof that good soup needn't be simmered all day on the back of a wood-burning stove. If you have the ingredients around, you can make this soup as fast as you could open a can.

Put all ingredients into a soup kettle, bring to a boil, and simmer gently for about 10 minutes. Serve hot.

Quick Turkey Soup

TIME: 30 MINUTES
YIELD: 6 SERVINGS
GOOD USE OF LEFTOVER TURKEY

¼ cup butter
¼ cup flour
6 cups turkey stock
¼ cup chopped fresh parsley
10 mushrooms, sliced
2 cups cooked barley or rice
1½ cups chopped cooked turkey
1 teaspoon soy sauce

Melt the butter in a soup kettle and gradually stir in the flour. Cook and stir over medium heat until the flour begins to brown slightly. Gradually stir in the turkey stock using a whisk, if necessary, to prevent lumps. Add the parsley, mushrooms, barley or rice, and turkey. Simmer all together for a few minutes to blend the flavors, then add the soy sauce. Serve at once.

Turkey Summer Squash Soup

TIME: 45 MINUTES, AFTER TURKEY
    IS COOKED
YIELD: 10 SERVINGS
GOOD USE OF LEFTOVER TURKEY

½ pound hot Italian sausage,
    sliced
1 large onion, sliced
4 cups canned or fresh tomatoes,
    cubed
1 medium-size zucchini, cubed
1 medium-size yellow crookneck
    squash, cubed
1 small pattypan squash, sliced
2 cups chopped cooked turkey
water as needed
salt to taste
yogurt

If you pour off the fat from the sausage in this recipe, it is quite a low-calorie soup, but wonderfully filling and a good way to use up cooked turkey and squash. Use all zucchini if you prefer.

In a soup kettle, fry the sausage until brown. Pour away as much of the fat as you can, and then sauté the onion until soft. Pour in the tomatoes and simmer, breaking up the tomatoes with a spoon. Add all the squash, cover the pan, and simmer for about 30 minutes, or until the squash is very tender. (This is not a recipe in which you try to keep the squash crisp.) Add the turkey and simmer for about 5 minutes longer. Add salt to taste. If the soup is too thick, add water. Serve topped with yogurt.

Variation
Substitute Italian sweet sausage for the hot, and add 1 teaspoon of caraway seeds when you sauté the onions.

Ground Turkey Chili

TIME: 2–3 HOURS, AFTER BEANS
  ARE COOKED (6–8 HOURS IN A
  SLOW COOKER)
YIELD: 8 SERVINGS
SLOW COOKER

Ground turkey is a wonderful bargain—about half the price of ground beef or veal—but unless you like meatloaf and meatballs, it's hard to find ways to use it. I was delighted that this chili turned out as well as any I've ever made. The turkey becomes sort of anonymous mixed in with all the spices. If you like chili extra hot, try a little extra cayenne pepper, cautiously.

I call this a soup, but served over corn bread it is hearty enough to make a satisfying main course.

1 tablespoon oil
1 large onion, chopped
½ green pepper, chopped
1 pound ground turkey (thawed if frozen)
1 cup tomato sauce or puree
4 cups canned tomatoes or fresh tomatoes, peeled and chopped
2 cups water
1 garlic clove, minced
2 tablespoons chili powder
1 teaspoon paprika
½ teaspoon dried oregano
½ teaspoon cumin
¼ teaspoon cayenne (or to taste)
2 cups cooked or canned pinto beans, drained
¾ cup corn masa flour or fine cornmeal mixed in ¾ cup cold water or 1 cup canned cream-style corn

Heat the oil in a heavy soup kettle or Dutch oven. Sauté the onion and pepper until soft. Add the ground turkey and brown it over medium high heat until it is separated into small pieces. (Turkey tends to stick together more than beef.) Add the tomato sauce, tomatoes, water, garlic, and spices. Reduce the heat to low, cover the kettle, and simmer for about an hour.

Add the beans and simmer at least another hour. Longer simmering improves the flavor.

Stir in the masa flour or cornmeal mixed in cold water, or the canned corn, and simmer all together, stirring occasionally, for about 15 minutes more. It doesn't matter which form of corn you use, for although the texture with each will be slightly different, the finished chili will have a faint "corny" taste with any of the three.

To prepare using a slow cooker, first heat the oil in a skillet and sauté the onion and peppers. Pour into the slow cooker. In the same skillet, brown the turkey and add that to the slow cooker. Add all other ingredients except the corn, cornmeal, or masa flour. *Use only 1 cup water*, rather than 2. Cover and cook on low for 6–8 hours. About 40 minutes before serving, turn the heat to high and stir in the corn, or cornmeal or masa flour mixed in water. Replace the lid and leave the heat under the chili on high until you serve it.

Turkey Minestrone

TIME: 1 HOUR, AFTER TURKEY
   AND BEANS ARE COOKED
YIELD: 12 SERVINGS
GOOD USE OF LEFTOVER TURKEY

2 quarts turkey stock
2 cups chopped cooked turkey
1 medium-size onion, chopped
1 celery rib, chopped
1 cup crushed tomatoes
1 cup chopped fresh zucchini (or
   any mixed vegetables)
1 cup cooked white beans
1 teaspoon salt
1 teaspoon chopped fresh thyme or
   ½ teaspoon dried
1 tablespoon chopped fresh parsley
   or 1½ teaspoons dried
2 cups fine dry noodles

Bring the stock to a boil in a soup kettle. Add the turkey, onion, celery, and tomatoes. Simmer for about 20 minutes. Add the zucchini, beans, salt, herbs, and noodles. Continue to simmer until the noodles are very soft and all the flavors have blended. For fun sometime, try using two different size noodles. Add the heavier ones first and stir in the finer ones a few minutes later. Serve hot.

Chicken
Main Dishes

When someone mentions poultry, most of us think first of chicken. The only person I know in the world who doesn't much like chicken is my father, who claims Grandmother Dietrick had it for so many Sunday dinners that he got tired of it. I wonder if maybe he got tired of the regular visits of Preacher and Mrs., not the chicken.

Eating chicken often doesn't have to be boring because you can vary the ways you cook it. Julia Child claims to have fed her husband chicken for dinner countless days in a row while she was testing recipes for poultry chapters in her various books without him ever complaining. And the Chinese count it a skill of the cook to be able to serve several chicken dishes in the same meal without seeming repetitious.

When Grandmother Dietrick was cooking chickens, she raised her own, butchered them shortly before she was ready to use them, and chose an old hen or a young hen according to how she wanted to cook it and how many people she needed to feed. If you raise your own chickens, you still have those options for freshness and quality. The choices for those of us who have to buy our chickens are pretty good, too. For a while it was hard to find any chicken in the grocery store that wasn't frozen; but recently, in addition to going whole hog in offering packages of chicken *parts* (if you'll forgive the mixed metaphor), chicken producers have improved packaging methods, which has increased the availability of fresh chicken. If it is fresh and properly stored, fresh chicken tastes better than frozen chicken; but a tightly wrapped, quick-frozen chicken kept frozen hard also can make a perfectly acceptable meal. Frozen chicken should not show signs of pink juice under the wrapping. This is a sign it has been partly thawed and refrozen, which means the chicken will be dry and tasteless.

CHICKENS BY CATEGORIES

To read the labels on chickens in the supermarket, you almost have to learn a second language. Here are the most common classifications.

Broilers–Fryers. These are very young, tender, and not too meaty. They usually weigh two to four pounds. Broilers and fryers are good cooked all ways.

Roasters. The grocery store equivalent to the old-fashioned *roasting hen,* roasters may occasionally be labeled by the second phrase. They weigh three to six pounds, have more fat, plumper breasts and thighs, and more flavor than broilers. Often they cost more per pound than broilers, but if you plan a traditional stuffed roast chicken, the roaster or roasting hen is the best choice.

Hens. Not to be confused with roasting hens, hens weigh as much as seven or eight pounds. Usually they are old and tough and good only for boiling for stock or making stewed chicken. Old hens cooked any other way will give you firsthand experience with the origins of the phrase, "she's a tough old bird."

Capons. Roosters that have been castrated to make them fatter are capons. They're the most expensive kind of chicken you can buy, purported to be more flavorful, but I'm not sure they are.

Chicken Parts. You can buy packages of all thighs, all drumsticks, all wings, and so on. That's straightforward enough, and comparing the price per pound on a package of wings and a package of drumsticks doesn't require special intelligence. But what about *drumettes* and *barbecue quarters* and *three-legged chickens?* Such novelty parts have become increasingly popular as more people eat more chicken and look for more ways to prepare it.

Novelty parts are fine as long as you know what you're getting. Drumettes are the first joint of the wings, with the tip joint removed.

They look like miniature drumsticks—hence the name—and cost more per pound than whole wings. Barbecue quarters are breast halves with the wings still on. Three-legged chickens are packages of cut-up chicken with an extra drumstick and thigh included. (The ones that make me mad are *three-neck* chickens with all three necks hidden underneath the regular parts.) In addition, you can buy cut-up chicken that has been disjointed in a variety of ways. Looking at the parts and reading the label are your best guides.

LOOK FOR SIGNS OF FRESHNESS

The labels on most packaged whole chickens and chicken parts carry dates. If the meat looks pinkish and not shriveled or dried out, and if the packaging material seems intact, you can be reasonably sure you are buying good chicken if the date on the label is current.

Should you find one of those rare places where chickens are sold on ice, unwrapped, look for firm flesh, unbroken and unbruised skin, and fresh (almost odorless) smell.

HOW TO CUT UP A CHICKEN

Cutting up your own chickens is worth learning, whether you raise them or buy them, because chicken parts are so versatile and because buying a whole chicken and cutting it up at home is almost always cheaper than buying parts.

I have read descriptions of how to cut up chickens which make it sound like you need a course in anatomy and another in engineering before you dare begin. Such nonsense. All you need to do is feel with your fingers to find each joint, then pull and bend to break it, and finally, cut through the flesh and broken joint. It works best to proceed systematically.

1. Cut off the legs by pulling each one away from the body.
2. Cut the thigh from the drumstick.
3. Cut the wings from the body as you did the legs.
4. Cut the back from the breast by running the knife along the ribs on each side.
5. If the breast is large, cut it in half by running the knife along the peak. The bone there is soft enough to allow you to cut through with firm pressure.

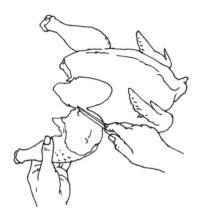

Cut off legs at thigh bone.

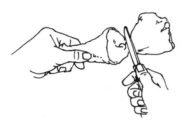

Cut thigh from drumstick.

Cut wings from body.

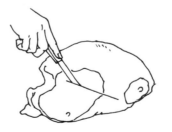

Cut back from breast along ribs.

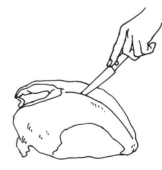

Cut breast in half along breast bone.

If you want chicken quarters for grilling or baking, leave the wings attached to the breast and the thighs attached to the drumstick.

HOW TO DEBONE A CHICKEN BREAST

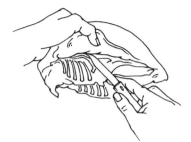

Scrape breast meat away from bones.

Some cookbooks make deboning chicken breasts sound so complicated you decide to give up white meat; but in fact all there is to it is using a thin, very sharp knife to slice and scrape the breast meat away from whatever bones it's attached to. Always cut so that you scrape in toward the bone, not into the good meat. Pull off the outer skin before you begin. And, again, try to be systematic. Start on one long edge and work around toward the other. You can pull some small bones away from the flesh with your fingers, without any cutting at all.

A WORD ABOUT THE CHICKEN RECIPES

Although recipes in this section specify various chicken parts, you don't have to take this too seriously. If the recipe says thighs and you happen to have legs, or quarters, go ahead and substitute. Or substitute a cut-up chicken for parts, or parts for cut-up chicken. The only case in which using the chicken part mentioned in a recipe *might* be important is when a delicate recipe uses chicken breasts, especially boned breasts. But even then you can always find a way to adapt the recipe to what you have. Just remember to increase or decrease the cooking time if the pieces you use are larger or smaller than those around which the recipe was designed.

Roast Chicken

Rinse the chicken thoroughly with cool water. Drain and dry with paper towels. Either stuff the chicken with a dressing or simply put a small, peeled onion and a piece of celery into the cavity. Tuck the legs under the flap of skin at the tail if it is intact, or tie them together with a piece of string. You may recall, as I do, your mother actually sewing the skin shut over the dressing. Later, it became fashionable to lace the bird shut by winding string around a series of long pins or skewers. None of this is necessary. The dressing at the cavity opening quickly browns and becomes crisp, sealing steam and moisture inside as effectively as all that trussing. If you're not comfortable with quite so casual an approach, wad up a piece of aluminum foil and fit it into the cavity opening.

Rub the chicken all over with oil or butter and place it in a flat baking pan. Roast according to either the high-temperature or low-temperature method.

Low-Temperature Method

Put the bird into a preheated 350°F. oven and roast, uncovered, for 18–20 minutes a pound (the lesser time is for unstuffed chicken), or until the leg moves easily in the socket and the chicken is nicely browned. Occasional basting with a little oil or melted butter makes the skin especially crisp, but it really isn't necessary.

High-Temperature Method

Prepare the chicken the same as with the low-temperature method. Roast in a preheated 450°F. oven, allowing about 15–18 minutes a pound. Baste occasionally, if you wish. The chicken is done when it is nicely browned, and the leg moves easily in the socket.

Proponents of the high-temperature method say it seals the juices in and produces a more tasty chicken. However, it also spatters the oven and sometimes fills the kitchen with smoke from the basting fat.

It's the Results That Count

If you use a meat thermometer, the chicken is done, by either method, when a thermometer stuck into the thickest part of the thigh registers about 170°F.

Some cooks like to place the chicken on a rack in its pan, to lift the bottom of the bird out of the accumulating juices and fat, and to allow the hot air to circulate more freely around the chicken as it roasts. You can do this, if you like. I have never been able to see that it made much difference one way or the other, especially since the *back* of the chicken usually goes for soup anyway.

Roasting a chicken can become as elaborate a ceremony as making stock, but it doesn't have to be. If you enjoy basting every few minutes, go ahead. It won't hurt and it might make a nicer-looking skin. But if you are busy with other things, an occasional basting after initially covering the chicken with oil or butter suffices—no matter what the French chefs say.

As for oven temperatures and timing, don't take any of it too seriously. If a 325°F. oven or a 425°F. oven suits your overall plan better, adjust the temperatures and add or subtract a little cooking time. In calculating cooking time by minutes-per-pound, remember that a larger chicken takes proportionately less time to roast than a smaller one. But don't worry about it. When it looks done, it probably is. After all, you're just roasting a chicken, not timing the reentry of a spacecraft into earth's atmosphere.

Making Gravy

If you're going all the way with this roast chicken project, you probably will want to serve mashed potatoes and gravy. Simple. Just lift the cooked chicken from the pan and set it aside to rest for about 15 minutes before `carving. Meanwhile, pour off all but about **4 tablespoons of the accumulated fat.** Put the pan on top of the stove and stir in about **4 tablespoons flour**—try to get about equal amounts of fat and flour. Cook and stir over medium heat until the flour begins to look slightly brown, then gradually whisk in hot stock or water, still cooking and stirring, until you have a mixture with a pleasing thickness. Allow about ¾ **cup water or stock** for each tablespoon of flour. Season with **salt** and a little **turmeric** to brighten up the color. If your gravy has lumps or big chunks of unidentifiable material from the cooking pan, strain through a sieve before serving.

Chicken or Turkey Hash (1 to 100)

TIME: 15 MINUTES
YIELD: 1 SERVING
GOOD USE OF LEFTOVERS

FOR EACH SERVING:

1 tablespoon butter
¼ cup chopped onion
¼ cup chopped green pepper
¼ cup chopped cooked potato
¼ cup chopped cooked vegetables
¼ cup chopped cooked chicken or
  other poultry
salt to taste
2 tablespoons water or stock, if
  needed

Melt the butter in a heavy skillet. Add the onion and green pepper and sauté until soft. Stir in the potato, vegetables, and chicken. Cook over medium heat without stirring again, until the mixture is brown and slightly crisp on the bottom. Add salt if desired. If the hash seems too dry, add a spoonful or so of water or stock. Serve with leftover gravy or a thin white sauce seasoned with mustard.

Chicken Bean Pot

TIME: 1 HOUR, AFTER THE BEANS
  ARE COOKED
YIELD: 6–8 SERVINGS
CLAY POT

½ **pound ground pork or sausage**
1 **celery rib, chopped**
1 **large onion, chopped**
½ **teaspoon salt**
¼ **teaspoon dried thyme**
¼ **teaspoon black pepper**
¼ **bay leaf**
2 **cups cooked white beans (small
  white or navy pea)**
4–5-**pound roasting chicken**
1 **garlic clove, unpeeled**
¼ **cup dry white wine**

Soak the clay pot in cold water for at least 15 minutes.

Fry the ground pork in a heavy skillet and drain off as much of the fat as possible. Add the chopped celery and onion and continue frying until the pork is in small pieces, and the onion and celery are soft. Stir in all seasonings, except the garlic.

Put the cooked beans in the bottom of the clay pot and stir the seasoned cooked pork into them.

Rinse the chicken in cold water, remove any chunks of fat you find, and put the chicken on top of the beans. Add the unpeeled garlic clove, leaving it where you can see it. Pour the white wine over all.

Cover the pot, place in a *cold* oven, and set the temperature at 450°F. Bake for 40–60 minutes, or until the chicken legs are just beginning to loosen in their sockets. If you pierce the thigh, the juice should be faintly pink. Open the pot away from you to avoid being burned by accumulated steam.

Remove the garlic. Cut the chicken into serving-size pieces and return them to the pot. Serve directly from the pot.

Thomas Jefferson's Chicken a la Merengo

TIME: 45 MINUTES
YIELD: 6 SERVINGS

Back in 1976 Marie Kimball published Thomas Jefferson's Cook Book, *in which she described the recipes he collected in his travels and the foods that his cooks prepared for his table. Apparently feeding the people who hung around with him took prodigious amounts of time and money. I have experimented with this chicken dish to standardize the measurements, but I am sure his cooks indulged in lots of leeway depending on what they had around and how many they had to feed. You can, too.*

4–5-pound chicken, cut up (or at least 6 pieces of assorted parts)
2 tablespoons oil
½ pound fresh mushrooms
salt to taste
1 clove garlic, minced
1 tablespoon chopped fresh parsley or 2 teaspoons dried
1 tablespoon chopped fresh or canned tomatoes
2 tablespoons stock
juice of 1 lemon
additional stock as needed

In a large skillet which has a tight-fitting lid, heat the oil and brown the chicken. Add the whole mushrooms and sauté briefly. Add salt to taste, garlic, parsley, tomatoes, stock, and lemon juice. Put on the lid and simmer over medium to low heat until the chicken is just cooked through, about 20 minutes. You may have to add a small amount of additional stock, but the idea is to steam the chicken in only a small amount of liquid so that when it is cooked, it seems more glazed than sauced. This dish is good hot or cold.

Grilled Picnic Chicken

TIME: 6–24 HOURS MARINATING;
    1 HOUR GRILLING
YIELD: 2 SERVINGS

1 small chicken (about 3 pounds)
⅓ cup red wine vinegar
⅓ cup salad oil
1 teaspoon dried tarragon
1 teaspoon dried basil
1 garlic clove

Take this to the beach or the woods and cook it over charcoal instead of steak or hamburgers.

Split the chicken in half, cutting through the peak of the breast and the back. For a more dramatic presentation, do not cut the back apart. This will leave you with a whole chicken that can be opened and spread flat on the grill.

Make a marinade by combining all the remaining ingredients. Do *not* add salt; the chicken will be juicier without it. Marinate the chicken in a large bowl or plastic bag in the refrigerator for 6–24 hours. If you use a plastic bag, you can carry the chicken to your picnic in it, marinade and all, if you slip it inside a second plastic bag to catch any leaks. Be sure to keep the chicken in a cooler until you are ready to cook it.

To cook, prepare the coals as you would for any other grilled meat; do not try to begin cooking until the coals are white all over. Spread the chicken flat on the grill, bony side down, and cook until the meat is almost done—about 40 minutes—before turning to cook the skin side. Baste occasionally with the marinade. An alternate method is to remove the grill and lay heavy aluminum foil directly on the hot coals. Place the chicken, bony side down, on the foil, cover with another piece of foil, and scatter some hot coals on top of that. This "top-bottom" cooking is a little faster and produces a wonderfully moist chicken.

Honey Barbecued Chicken

TIME: 2–12 HOURS MARINATING;
  45–50 MINUTES GRILLING
YIELD: 6 SERVINGS

**8-ounce can tomato sauce or 1 cup
  tomato puree**
½ cup oil
½ cup orange juice
¼ cup cider vinegar
1½ teaspoons dried oregano
½ teaspoon salt
1 garlic clove, mashed
**1 cut-up chicken or any assortment
  of pieces**
¼ cup honey
½ teaspoon dry mustard
1 tablespoon butter, melted

*If you begin marinating the chicken and prepare the barbecue glaze the
night before, cooking this the next day is practically effortless.*

Combine the tomato sauce, oil, orange juice, vinegar, oregano, garlic,
and salt. Marinate the chicken in the mixture for 2–12 hours
refrigerated. Turn the pieces occasionally to be sure all are coated.

To prepare the glaze, combine the honey, mustard, and melted
butter. This is easiest to do if you first warm the honey slightly.

When you are ready to cook, light the charcoal and allow to burn
until all the coals are white. Arrange the chicken on the grill and cook
for 45–50 minutes, turning often and brushing with the marinade.
During the last 5 minutes of cooking, brush with the honey glaze.
Serve with corn-on-the-cob and salad.

Classic Southern Fried Chicken

TIME: 45 MINUTES
YIELD: 6 SERVINGS

As far as I am concerned, anybody who eats like this should fast the day before and take an EKG the day afterwards. But Southern Fried Chicken is so much a part of American mythology I didn't dare leave it out. This recipe, which I found in the Savannah Cookbook, *by Harriet Ross Colquit, is a classic. The original directions were somewhat less specific than those here, presumably because everyone was already familiar with Southern Fried Chicken. Although the book was published back in 1933, I've had to run off enough calories since moving south to testify that Southerners still prepare chicken this way.*

The only possible way to serve Fried Chicken is with heaps of mashed potatoes heavily seasoned with butter and black pepper.

1 large chicken, cut up, or
  6–8 pieces of assorted chicken
  parts
1 cup flour
oil for deep frying
1 heaping tablespoon flour
½ cup cream
¼ teaspoon pepper
salt to taste

Coat each piece of chicken with flour while you are heating the fat in a deep, heavy skillet. (Once lard would have been the frying fat; I suggest vegetable oil.) The fat should be hot enough to brown a bread cube when you drop it in; fat that is too cool makes greasy fried chicken. Fry the chicken pieces, a few at a time, in the deep fat until the chicken is well browned on the outside and done through. Set the chicken aside and keep it warm while you make the gravy.

To make the gravy, pour off all but about 1 tablespoon of the fat. Stir the tablespoon of flour into the drippings remaining in the skillet, and cook and stir until the flour turns golden brown. Remove the pan from the heat. Gradually stir in the cream, using a whisk if necessary to prevent lumps. Heat thoroughly, but do not return to a boil. Pour this gravy over the chicken and serve immediately.

Variations

Some cooks dip the chicken in beaten egg before dredging with flour; some brown the chicken quickly in the fat and then bake it in a flat pan in a 300°F. oven for 30–45 minutes, or until done through. This works well if you are feeding a large group. To make Southern Fried Chicken for a picnic, omit the gravy.

Crisp Baked Chicken

TIME: 1 HOUR
YIELD: 6 SERVINGS

6 chicken quarters
1 cup buttermilk
3 heaping cups wheat flakes or
   cornflakes

When I first heard about using buttermilk to bind the coating for baked chicken, I was skeptical; but this has become one of my favorite recipes. It's as good cold as it is hot and is perfect for picnics.

Preheat the oven to 350°F.

Dip the chicken quarters into the buttermilk, and set aside briefly while you crush the cereal flakes. Then dip the chicken into the flakes, and lay the chicken on a flat pan or cookie sheet far enough apart so that the pieces do not touch each other, skin side up. Bake for 1 hour. Serve hot or cold.

The Tavern's Steam-Baked Chicken

TIME: 15 MINUTES BREADING
  AND FRYING; 1 HOUR BAKING
YIELD: 6 SERVINGS

3 eggs
½ teaspoon salt
¼ teaspoon pepper
¼ teaspoon celery salt
6 small chicken breasts or 3 large,
  split
2 cups flour
oil for frying

My husband learned how to make this chicken years ago when he worked as a waiter at The Tavern in New Wilmington, Pennsylvania, which was famous for its chicken. His version is a simplification of the large-scale methods used in the Tavern. Unless you have an ovenproof steamer, you'll have to rig up something with racks and baking pans, as we do.

Beat the eggs in a bowl large enough to hold a chicken breast. Add the seasonings. Pull the skin off the breasts and dip each piece of chicken into the eggs; then roll in the flour until completely coated.

Preheat the oven to 350°F.

Heat 1–1½ inches of oil in a large skillet and fry the chicken breasts, a few at a time, until browned on all sides, about 7 minutes. Arrange the browned chicken on a rack and place over hot water in any pan large enough to support the rack. Cover the chicken with wet cheesecloth or a wet dish towel and steam-bake for 1 hour. If the wet cloth dries out, sprinkle extra water on it at least once during the hour.

Serve with a green vegetable or grilled tomato.

Chicken and Shrimp for a Party

TIME: 45 MINUTES PREPARING;
  35–45 MINUTES REHEATING
YIELD: 6 SERVINGS
MICROWAVE OVEN

2 pounds boneless chicken breasts
  (about 8 pieces)
1 cup flour
1½ cups stock
2 tablespoons butter
2 tablespoons oil
1 tablespoon flour
1 bay leaf
1 tablespoon tomato paste
salt to taste
⅓ cup dry white wine
½ pound large shrimp, cooked and
  peeled
2 fresh peeled or whole canned
  tomatoes, quartered
1 tablespoon chopped fresh parsley

Consider this a party dish, because the shrimp makes it expensive, and because it requires a little more time to prepare than most of us can devote to everyday meals. You can prepare everything ahead and just heat it through on a baking dish at serving time with excellent results. This combination is good served with a cucumber salad and steamed asparagus.

Dredge the chicken breasts in 1 cup flour. Heat the stock and keep it warm.

In a heavy skillet, melt the butter and oil together. Add the chicken breasts and sauté over medium-high heat until the breasts are brown on both sides and just cooked through, about 15 minutes. Set aside. Into the skillet, stir in 1 tablespoon flour to make a thin roux (paste), and then whisk in the hot stock, stirring rapidly to prevent lumps. Continue cooking and stirring until the mixture has thickened into a gravy. Season with the bay leaf, tomato paste, salt, and wine.

To serve, arrange the chicken breasts on a baking dish. Arrange the shrimp and tomato quarters on top. Pour the sauce over all, and heat in a 450°F. oven for about 45 minutes, or until heated through. Or heat in a glass baking dish in a microwave oven, at a medium-high setting. Run the microwave about 5 minutes at a time until the chicken is heated through. Be careful not to overcook. Sprinkle with parsley just before serving.

Chicken Breasts With Zucchini

TIME: 1 HOUR
YIELD: 6 SERVINGS
CLAY POT

2 medium-size (8–10-inch)
  zucchini
3 large chicken breasts,
  split in half
¼ cup catsup
1 tablespoon brown sugar
1 tablespoon cider vinegar
½ teaspoon prepared mustard

A recipe so easy you almost feel guilty about accepting the compliments it brings. Good served with noodles.

Soak the clay pot in cold water for at least 15 minutes.

Slice the zucchini into 1-inch slices; do not peel first. Place the zucchini in the clay pot. Arrange the chicken breasts over the zucchini. You may have to squeeze them to make them fit. It doesn't matter. Mix together the catsup, brown sugar, vinegar, and mustard. Pour over the chicken breasts.

Put the cover on the pot and place in a *cold* oven. Turn the heat to 475°F. and bake for 30–40 minutes. The breasts should be moist and tender. Do not overcook. You will find the zucchini somewhat softer than if you had cooked it separately, but it will taste wonderful.

To prepare this without a clay pot, bake in a covered casserole in a preheated 350°F. oven for about 1 hour. Check once or twice to see if you need to add a little water.

Chicken Breasts With Chinese Vegetables

TIME: 1 HOUR BAKING CHICKEN
   BREASTS; 10 MINUTES STIR
   FRYING
YIELD: 6 SERVINGS
CLAY POT

3 large or 6 small chicken breasts
¼ cup water or stock
2–4 tablespoons vegetable oil
1 green pepper, sliced
4 cups broccoli florets
20 scallions, sliced
6 mushrooms, sliced
2 cups bean sprouts
8-ounce can water chestnuts,
   drained and sliced
liquid from cooking the chicken
   plus enough water or stock to
   make 1 cup
1 tablespoon soy sauce
1 tablespoon cornstarch
¼ cup cold water

I can't imagine anyone not liking this. It makes a fine company meal since the only last minute cooking is stir frying the vegetables, which takes only a few minutes.

Soak the clay pot in cold water for at least 15 minutes before using.

Split the breasts if they are large. Arrange the chicken breasts in the pot. Add ¼ cup water or stock. Put the cover on and place the pot in a *cold* oven. Turn the heat to 475°F. and bake for 50–60 minutes, or until chicken is tender, but still juicy. Open the clay pot away from you to make sure you are not burned by escaping steam. (If you are not using a clay pot, cook the breasts by any other method you like.)

To cook the vegetables, heat a tablespoon of the oil in the bottom of a wok or large frying pan until almost, but not quite, smoking. Add the vegetables, in the order listed, stirring and cooking over high heat until the broccoli is tender crisp. Add the cup of cooking liquid and bring quickly to a boil. Add the soy sauce. Combine the cornstarch and water and stir into the wok. Continue cooking just until the sauce loses its cloudiness and its starchy taste.

Arrange the chicken breasts on a serving platter and pour the vegetables over them. Serve with rice.

Chicken Breasts in Sherry

TIME: 1 HOUR
YIELD: 6 SERVINGS

½ cup flour
salt and pepper to taste
¼ teaspoon paprika
6 small or 3 large chicken breasts
½ cup oil
½ cup dry sherry
dried whole rosemary, crushed

This is easy but special enough for a party. To serve a crowd, just keep increasing the number of chicken breasts and add the other ingredients in greater quantity as you need them. Don't worry too much about the proportions.

Preheat the oven to 350°F.

Combine the flour, salt, pepper, and paprika. Split the breasts if they are large. Coat the chicken breasts with the seasoned flour. Heat the oil in a heavy skillet and fry the chicken in it until brown and crisp on the outside. Remove the chicken from the skillet and place in a single layer in a shallow baking pan. Pour the sherry over the breasts and sprinkle them with crushed rosemary. Cover the pan with aluminum foil, crimping it against the edges. Bake in the preheated oven for 40–50 minutes, or until the chicken is tender. Do not overcook. Serve with green peas and rice, pouring any remaining pan juices over the breasts.

Chicken in Pudding

TIME: 1¼ HOURS
YIELD: 6 SERVINGS
BLENDER

6 small or 3 large chicken breasts
¼ cup stock or white wine
4 eggs
1 cup milk
1 cup flour
½ teaspoon baking powder
salt to taste

Elegant and old-fashioned, the pudding has overtones of Yorkshire pudding baked around roast beef.

Preheat the oven to 350°F.

If you use the large breasts, split them in half. Put the stock or wine in the bottom of a pan with a tight-fitting lid. Bring to a boil, add the breasts, cover tightly, and steam over medium heat for about 15 minutes. The liquid should be almost entirely evaporated. If it evaporates too fast, add a spoonful or so of water as needed. Cook until the chicken is *almost* done. Pull the skin off the breasts and arrange the breasts in a single layer in a greased baking dish.

In the blender (or a bowl), beat together the eggs, milk, flour, baking powder, and salt until very smooth. Pour this mixture over the chicken and bake in the preheated oven for about 1 hour, or until the pudding is puffed and brown and the chicken is done through. Serve each piece of chicken with some of the pudding.

Soy Sauce Chicken

TIME: 40 MINUTES
YIELD: 6 SERVINGS

Soy sauce and chicken may be the perfect combination. The soy sauce mixture in which you cook the chicken may be refrigerated and used over again.

6 small or 3 large chicken breasts
1 cup soy sauce
1 cup water
½ cup brown sugar
1 cup dry sherry
4 scallions, sliced

If you are using large breasts, split each one in half. In a skillet broad enough to hold all the breasts in a single layer, bring the soy sauce, water, brown sugar, sherry, and scallions to a boil. Put the breasts into the hot liquid and cover. Cook over moderate heat for about 35 minutes, turning the breasts occasionally so the sauce is absorbed evenly.

Remove the chicken from the sauce and cool the sauce before serving. For elegant service, slice the meat from the breasts or pull out the bone to serve them boneless. Discard the skin. Serve at room temperature.

To reuse the soy sauce mixture, refresh it with a little more sherry, sugar, and soy sauce in the same proportions as you made it originally.

Soy Sauce Chicken II

TIME: 6–8 HOURS
YIELD: 4–6 SERVINGS
SLOW COOKER

Here is a simpler version of Soy Sauce Chicken prepared in a slow cooker.

3–4 pounds chicken parts
1 large onion, sliced
¼ cup soy sauce
¾ cup water
1 tablespoon sugar

Place the chicken parts in the slow cooker. Push the onion slices down around the sides. Mix the soy sauce, water, and sugar. Pour over the chicken. Cover the pot and cook on low for 6–8 hours. Before serving, remove the chicken skin and the bones. Serve over rice with a few spoonfuls of the sauce.

Spiced Chicken

TIME: 45 MINUTES
YIELD: 6 SERVINGS

1 cup orange juice
1½ cups sliced peaches (fresh,
   canned, or frozen)
2 tablespoons brown sugar
2 tablespoons cider vinegar
½ teaspoon nutmeg
1 teaspoon chopped fresh basil or
   ½ teaspoon dried
1 garlic clove, mashed
½ cup flour
salt to taste
6 chicken legs and thighs,
   not cut apart
vegetable oil for frying

In a saucepan, mix the orange juice, peaches, brown sugar, vinegar, nutmeg, basil, and garlic. Bring to a boil and simmer for 10 minutes.

Combine the flour and salt. Roll the chicken in the flour. Heat the oil in a large, heavy skillet. Add the chicken. When the chicken is nicely browned, drain it on paper towels. It does not need to be cooked all the way through. Pour off all the oil from the skillet, but leave the browned flour and dried chicken bits. Return the chicken to the skillet, pour the fruit mixture on top, cover the pan, and simmer gently for about 20 mintues, or until the chicken is just cooked through. Serve with rice.

Variations

Substitute pineapple for the peaches. Substitute lemon juice and cinnamon for the vinegar and nutmeg.

Thicken the sauce by combining 1 tablespoon cornstarch with 2 tablespoons water and stirring into the sauce during the last few minutes of cooking.

Use a whole cut-up chicken (about 3 pounds) instead of the legs and thighs.

Greek-Style Baked Chicken (1 to 100)

TIME: 1 HOUR
YIELD: 1 SERVING

Easy, but good enough for a party. Maintain the Greek tone by serving with eggplant in tomato sauce, mashed chick peas, and green salad with feta cheese, or keep it simple by serving with potatoes baked at the same time as the chicken and steamed green beans.

FOR EACH SERVING:

1 tablespoon olive oil
1 tablespoon red wine or red wine
  vinegar
1 tablespoon chopped fresh parsley
½ teaspoon minced fresh thyme or
¼ teaspoon dried
1 tablespoon minced green onion
salt to taste (optional)
1 chicken quarter

Preheat the oven to 350°F.

Combine the oil, wine, herbs, onion, and salt. Rub each piece of chicken with the mixture. Place the chicken pieces so they are not touching each other in a large, flat pan. Bake uncovered for 1 hour. Serve hot.

Chicken and Barley Stew

TIME: 2 HOURS
YIELD: 6 SERVINGS

6 chicken legs or thighs,
  or a combination of both
2 medium-size onions, chopped
1 celery rib, chopped
1 carrot, chopped
1 small ham slice, chopped, or
  about 1 cup leftover ham pieces
1 cup dry white wine
1½ cups canned or fresh peeled
  tomatoes
1 garlic clove, minced
½ cup uncooked barley
3 tablespoons chopped fresh
  parsley or 1 tablespoon dried
1 teaspoon chopped fresh thyme or
  ½ teaspoon dried
salt to taste

You don't have to use legs and thighs for this stew, but I think the dark meat has better flavor and texture in this recipe than white meat. You won't need anything more than a green salad to make this stew a complete meal.

In a heavy Dutch oven or stew pot, brown the chicken slowly. If you start with a moderately hot pan, there should be enough fat under the skin of the chicken so you need no extra fat. As the legs and thighs finish browning, stir in the onions, celery, and carrot, and cook them along with the chicken until they begin to soften slightly. Add the ham, wine, tomatoes, and garlic, and bring to a boil. Stir in the barley, parsley, and thyme. Reduce the heat so that the stew simmers gently, with bubbles barely showing on top. Cover and simmer about 1½ hours, until the chicken is very tender. Prepared this way, the barley will be very soft. If you prefer a firmer grain, allow the stew to simmer for about 30 minutes before stirring in the barley. Add salt to taste and serve.

Simple Oriental-Style Baked Chicken

TIME: 15 MINUTES MARINATING;
   50 MINUTES BAKING
YIELD: 6 SERVINGS

6 chicken quarters
¼ cup soy sauce
1 slice fresh ginger root, minced, or
substitute a pinch of powdered
ginger
1 garlic clove, mashed
¼ cup orange marmalade
2 tablespoons soy sauce
2 tablespoons water
toasted sesame oil (optional)

Arrange the chicken quarters in a flat baking pan so the pieces are not touching each other. Mix the ¼ cup soy sauce, ginger, and garlic, and pour the mixture over the chicken, rubbing it into the pieces with your fingers. Allow to stand at a cool room temperature for 15 minutes. Cover the pan with aluminum foil, sealing the edges tightly. Place the pan in the oven and turn the heat to 350°F. Bake for about 40 minutes, or until the chicken is tender. Remove the foil.

Mix together the marmalade, 2 tablespoons soy sauce, the water, and a few drops of sesame oil if you are using it. Reset the oven to 450°F. Brush the chicken with the marmalade sauce and return the pan to the oven for 5–10 minutes, just long enough to brown the tops of the chicken quarters.

Steamed snow peas and rice go perfectly with this chicken.

Chicken Bordeaux

TIME: 1 HOUR
YIELD: 6 SERVINGS

6 chicken thighs
¼ cup flour
2 tablespoons oil
2 tablespoons butter
1 large onion, chopped
1 large carrot, chopped
1 celery rib, chopped
1 garlic clove, mashed
1 cup red Bordeaux wine
1 teaspoon chopped fresh thyme or
   ½ teaspoon dried
¼ bay leaf
½ cup water or stock
2 medium-size unpeeled red
   potatoes, sliced

This may be my favorite recipe in the whole book. It is one of the few in which no substitute for the wine will produce even remotely similar results.

Roll the chicken pieces in the flour. In a heavy stove-top casserole or Dutch oven, heat the oil and butter and sauté the onion, celery, and garlic until all but the carrots are soft, but not brown. Remove them from the pan and lightly brown the floured chicken pieces. You may need to add a little more oil. Return the sautéed vegetables to the pan, pour in the wine, and add the herbs and the water. Arrange the sliced potatoes on top so they are not soaking in the liquids. Bring to a boil, reduce the heat, cover the casserole with a close-fitting lid, and simmer for 40 minutes.

Everything that makes a meal is already in the pot. You could serve with some green peas or a sharply seasoned spinach salad for one of the all-time great dinners.

Italian Chicken Casserole

TIME: 15 MINUTES FOR SAUCE
  AND MACARONI; 1½ HOURS
  BAKING
YIELD: 8–10 SERVINGS
GOOD USE OF LEFTOVER CHICKEN

Lasagna is the inspiration for this casserole, but this is much simpler to make. It needs nothing more than a green salad to be a hearty meal. You could substitute turkey for the chicken.

8 ounces uncooked macaroni twists
  (or other pasta shape)
5 cups tomato sauce or tomato
  puree
1½ teaspoons fresh basil or
  ½ teaspoon dried
1½ teaspoons fresh oregano or
  ½ teaspoon dried
1 tablespoon chopped fresh parsley
1 garlic clove, minced
1 onion slice, minced
1 tablespoon olive oil
½ cup grated cheese (preferably
  provolone or mozzarella)
1 pound ricotta or small-curd
  cottage cheese
nutmeg
salt to taste
2 eggs
1 cup finely chopped cooked
  chicken
5 small (4–6-inch) zucchini, sliced

Cook the macaroni in boiling water according to package instructions until it is barely done. Drain and set aside.

Preheat the oven to 350°F. Mix the tomato sauce with the herbs, garlic, onion, and olive oil in a small pan, and simmer together for 15 minutes.

Combine the grated cheese and ricotta with a sprinkle of nutmeg and salt. Beat in the eggs. Stir in the chicken.

Spread about 2 cups of the tomato sauce in the bottom of a large oiled casserole or lasagna pan. Put a layer of macaroni over that. Cover with a layer of zucchini. Pour the cheese-chicken mixture over the zucchini, and pour the remaining tomato sauce over all.

Cover the casserole with a lid or aluminum foil and bake for 1½ hours, or until the contents of the pan are bubbling all through. Serve hot.

Quick Italian-Style Chicken With Spaghetti

TIME: 15 MINUTES, AFTER
  SPAGHETTI IS COOKED
YIELD: 6 SERVINGS
GOOD USE OF LEFTOVER CHICKEN

2 tablespoons olive oil
2 onions, cubed
1 green pepper, cubed
4 cups cooked or canned tomatoes
½ teaspoon pepper
salt to taste
2 cups chopped cooked chicken
4 cups leftover cooked spaghetti or
  ½ pound cooked fresh

I invented this recipe one night after work when I was hungry, in a hurry, and faced with a refrigerator full of leftovers. It tastes so delicious people think it requires hours of work. Cutting the ingredients in large chunks speeds preparation and adds distinctive character to the dish.

In a heavy skillet, heat the olive oil. Sauté the onion and green pepper long enough to soften them. Add the canned tomatoes, pepper, and salt. Cook down fast, stirring almost constantly, until about half the juice is evaporated. This will take 5–10 minutes. Add the chicken and the cooked spaghetti. Stir all together and continue cooking just until everything is hot again. Don't overcook the spaghetti in the sauce or it will be gummy. Serve at once.

Home-Style Chicken Salad

TIME: ABOUT 10 MINUTES IF THE
CHICKEN, DRESSING, AND
MAYONNAISE HAVE ALREADY
BEEN PREPARED
YIELD: 4 SERVINGS
GOOD USE OF LEFTOVER CHICKEN

2 cups coarsely chopped cooked
  chicken
½ cup chopped celery
¼ cup chopped sweet onion
½ cup Boiled Dressing (page 111)
½ cup Mayonnaise (page 110)
3 hard-boiled eggs, chopped
salt or vinegar to taste

This is just about the only chicken salad I like; most others are too bland. The Boiled Dressing is what produces the extra flavor. Instead of chicken salad sandwiches, try serving this with romaine lettuce and cold marinated vegetables.

In a large bowl, combine the chicken, celery, and onion. In a separate bowl, stir together the Boiled Dressing and Mayonnaise, thinning with a little water if the mixture seems too thick. Pour over the chicken and vegetables, mixing gently. Add the chopped eggs and stir just enough to mix them in. Do not mix so hard that you mush up the pieces of egg.

If you add about 1 teaspoon vinegar to the mayonnaise-dressing mix, this salad is tasty without salt.

Chinese Chicken Livers

TIME: 3 HOURS MARINATING;
   5 MINUTES COOKING
YIELD: 4–6 SERVINGS

I used to wonder why chicken livers are available in such large quantities in grocery stores; then somebody observed that after packaging all those chicken parts, the marketers had to do something with the livers that originally came with each chicken. If you raise your own chickens and use only one or two at a time, you can accumulate enough livers to cook separately by freezing them.

1 quart water
1 pound chicken livers
3 tablespoons soy sauce
1 tablespoon sherry
1 tablespoon brown sugar
½ teaspoon salt
1 garlic clove, minced
2 tablespoons oil

Bring the water to a boil and drop in the chicken livers. Parboil for about 2 minutes. Drain. Mix all the remaining ingredients, but the oil, and refrigerate the livers in the marinade for 3 hours.

Just before serving time, dry the livers on paper towels, heat the oil in a heavy skillet, and toss the livers into the hot oil. Sauté over fairly high heat for about 2 minutes, stirring or shaking the pan, until the livers are just cooked through. Be sure to wear an apron in this step because the moisture in the livers causes them to spatter when they hit the hot oil. Serve warm.

Main Dish Turkeys

People are intimidated by turkeys. Alive, they're fierce-looking birds that seem aggressive enough to remove your exposed toes if you get near them wearing sandals. Dressed and raw, they challenge you to figure out how to cook them and for how long. Cooked, they dominate the dinner table until someone works up the courage to carve.

The thing to remember in every phase is that you are bigger than that bird.

If you raise your own turkeys, handle butchering and dressing exactly as you would a chicken. Buying a turkey is a little more complicated than buying chicken, because so many more things are being done to the basic bird.

Most of the turkeys available these days are frozen, except at holiday time. And many of the frozen turkeys are called "self-basting" or "prebasted." A mixture of coconut oil, butter, or a water-carried seasoning is introduced into the breast meat without puncturing the skin. The label must tell you what the basting mixture contains. Although these prebasted turkeys are increasingly popular and have saved careless cooks from enough disasters to warrant repeat purchases, purists will insist their taste can't match that of a well-prepared fresh turkey.

What's more, the price on the prebasted varieties is several cents a pound more. I bought one recently when I couldn't find any other kind in the size I wanted, and was dumbfounded when I started preparing it to discover inside the bird's cavity an assortment of strings, plastic pins, and a little button that was supposed to pop up when the turkey was done. For the cost of all that gadgetry, I thought, I could have bought another pound of real turkey.

If you look long enough in the freezer case, or ask the butcher in the grocery store, you can find frozen turkeys which have not been treated in any way beyond dressing and quick-freezing. If they have been stored properly and do not look dried out under the plastic wrap, these turkeys are excellent.

Better yet, when you can find one, is a fresh turkey. The taste and texture are significantly better. A grocery-store fresh turkey is a pretty safe bet. If you buy one, dressed, from a farmer or in a country market, check it closely to be sure it smells fresh, has firm flesh, and does not appear bruised or purplish in spots from inexpert slaughtering. A lot of trouble, but worth it.

No matter what kind of turkey you buy, a young one is better than an old one. And not all *small* turkeys are necessarily young. Some are being bred for smaller size; others may simply be a poorer grade. Some may have had their growth stunted by poor diet or bad living conditions. The law requires that turkeys are inspected for wholesomeness; the inspection mark is round. Some turkeys are also graded. Grading is voluntary; the mark is a shield shape. You are more likely to find such grading on frozen than on fresh turkeys. I am not convinced that the actual difference between the higher and lower grades amounts to much. Some cooks familiar with game cookery recommend that a fresh turkey rest a day or two in the refrigerator before cooking to allow the muscle tissue to relax. I suspect this applies only to turkeys bought directly from a farmer; those in the grocery store have had plenty of time to relax in the display case.

If the turkey is frozen, you will get the best results by thawing it slowly—two or three days in its wrapper in the refrigerator, depending on its size. Thawing at room temperature can be dangerous in warm weather. The packer's suggestion that you thaw the turkey under cold running water sounds great but becomes a nuisance when you actually try to do it. Don't bother to thaw the turkey in the microwave or to cook it before it's fully defrosted. The meat will be dry, stringy, and tasteless enough to give turkey a bad name it doesn't deserve.

THE BASIC ROAST TURKEY

Once ready for cooking, the basic roast turkey can be done in as many different ways as there are cooks. Essentially, you either roast it covered or uncovered. If you use a cover, you are really steaming it. This is best for a very large bird, an old bird, or a game bird (wild turkey).

Dry roasting at low heat works well for young, tender birds, especially if you take care to baste occasionally.

Aluminum foil and ingenuity have produced a couple of variations on these basic methods. The loose tent of foil laid across the breast of the turkey gives a sort of combination steam-roast cooking which still lets the turkey brown nicely, while making basting unnecessary.

Another variation is to roast the turkey *breast-side-down* for most of the cooking period, turning it over for only the last half hour or so. This definitely produces juicier white meat, but the finished turkey looks less handsome if you want to carry it whole to the table. And when you are dealing with a twenty-pound turkey, the turning-over process is hazardous enough to make you worry about your investment. One way to handle it is to confine your kitchen help to people you trust not to tattle. Then, if the whole thing falls on the floor, you can pick it up, wipe it off, and the two of you can keep the secret.

We tend to overcook turkey, no matter how we roast it. If it is falling off the bones, as our grandmothers used to like to say, it is too done. The leg should just move easily in its socket, and the juice from the thigh should be faintly pink when you pierce the thigh with a fork.

THE CHALLENGE
OF TURKEY PARTS AND LEFTOVERS

Overcooking is less of a problem with the introduction of turkey parts, cut and packaged somewhat like chicken parts. The challenge of these, except perhaps for the breast, is finding ways to use them. A pair of raw turkey legs and thighs intimidates me until I remind myself that it's *my* kitchen and the turkey is only visiting.

Intimidation inheres in turkey leftovers, too. Look at the splash of recipes in your newspaper around Thanksgiving and you get the feeling cooks everywhere are trying to reassure each other that it's possible to make good meals out of the other half of the 22-pound holiday spectacular. What pays off with leftovers as bland as turkey meat is a devil-may-care slinging together of the available ingredients. Turkey hash concocted the same way you'd put together a beef hash is especially good. The thing to remember in inventing turkey concoctions is that you weren't ultimately intimidated by the bird in its full-sized glory; nor should you be intimidated by its bony remains.

TIMING ROAST TURKEY

Every cookbook I have ever looked in has suggested a different timetable for roasting turkey. The following is the one recommended by a marketer of brand-name turkeys. These turkeys are roasted in a 375°F. oven.

Roasting Times

Size of Turkey	Unstuffed	Stuffed
4–7 pounds	1½–2 hours	1¾–2 hours
1–10 pounds	2–2 ½ hours	2½–3 hours

Larger turkeys are frequently roasted at the more common 325°F. temperature.

Size of Turkey	Unstuffed	Stuffed
12–16 pounds	3–4 hours	3½–4½ hours
16–20 pounds	4–5 ½ hours	4–6 hours

When the turkey is "done," the temperature of the thigh on a meat thermometer should be 180–185°F. at the thickest part; the internal temperature of a stuffed turkey should register 160–165°F. in the stuffing.

To complicate all this timing further, a turkey will cook faster in a dark roasting pan than in a light one, and a heavy breasted turkey will take longer than a long skinny one.

I think the easiest way to approach all this is to roast the turkey in a 325°F. oven, or possibly a 350°F. oven, allowing *about* 20 minutes a pound. When the turkey looks brown all over, the thigh lets out yellow rather than pink juice if pierced, and the leg moves easily in its socket, the turkey is done. Since the turkey needs to stand a few minutes, up to half an hour, before being carved, you can relax and let it be done a little earlier than you've planned for the rest of the meal and everything works out beautifully.

ABOUT STUFFING TURKEY

I grew up thinking that the only way to stuff turkey was with a dressing made of dried bread. If my Grandmother Dietrick made it, it was a highly seasoned stuffing with lots of herbs, onion, and celery. If Grandmother Pennington made it, it was soft and bland, without onion or any strident seasonings. Each had its virtues. Grandma Dietrick's was great warmed over for breakfast, with a couple of fried eggs; Grandma Pennington's was perfect for serving with lots of hot, salty giblet gravy. For years it haunted me that, even using their recipes, I couldn't duplicate the dressings. Eventually I realized the problem was the *bread*. Most of the old-time dressing recipes were developed for using up dried, stale bread. In fact, one great comedy routine by Bob and Ray is about how the first Thanksgiving turkey was a wild, scrawny thing, and one of them said to the other, "That's okay, stuff it full of old bread so it won't look so skinny."

Today's store-bought bread just isn't equal to the task. When it gets stale, it crumples to nothing, and attempts to reconstitute it by pouring on hot water and then squeezing the bread dry, as in the old recipes, produce a pasty mess that craftspeople use for making little miniature plants and food for doll houses, but that isn't good for much else. The moral is, don't even think of trying bread stuffing unless you've got good bread.

The traditional way to bake the stuffing was to fill the cavity of the bird with the stuffing, then lace the cavity shut with a big needle and string. Eventually, trussing pins or skewers, which you stuck into the breast skin and laced up kind of like hiking boots, came into vogue. In truth, you need neither. Just tie the legs together with a bit of string, or stick a wad of aluminum foil in the opening of the cavity. Or do nothing. The reason for the elaborate trussing was to seal moisture and juices inside the bird, but the roasting does this naturally by forming a toasted crust over whatever stuffing is exposed. That works just fine to seal in as much moisture as most stuffings need

Bread Stuffing

TIME: 30 MINUTES
YIELD: ABOUT 4 CUPS STUFFING,
    ENOUGH TO STUFF A
    9–12-POUND TURKEY

4 cups stale bread cubes
¼ cup butter or 2 tablespoons oil
    and 2 tablespoons butter
1 large onion, chopped
1 celery rib, chopped
¼ cup chopped fresh parsley or
    2 tablespoons dried
1 teaspoon chopped fresh thyme or
    ¼ teaspoon dried
3 eggs
salt and pepper to taste

Don't try this unless you have homemade bread or something similar from a natural foods store.

Put the bread cubes into a large mixing bowl. Melt the butter in a large skillet and sauté the onion and celery. Stir in the parsley and thyme. Pour into the bread cubes and mix well. Beat the eggs lightly and add them to the bread cubes. Mix. Season with salt and pepper and stuff into the cavity of the turkey. The stuffing will seem somewhat dry, but the moisture from the roasting bird will give it a perfect consistency by the time you have finished roasting the turkey in your usual manner.

German Potato Stuffing

TIME: 1½ HOURS BAKING
  POTATOES; 15 MINUTES
  ASSEMBLING
YIELD: 3–4 CUPS, ENOUGH TO
  STUFF A 9–12-POUND TURKEY

3 large baking potatoes
4 slices bacon
6 green onions
1 tablespoon sugar
1 tablespoon cider vinegar
salt and pepper to taste

I developed this recipe especially for this cookbook, and I had lots of trouble with it. First problem was that it tasted so good I had trouble getting it into the turkey without eating too much of it. Then, at dinner, everybody liked it so well, they ate a lot of it, consuming much less turkey than usual. And worst of all, the next morning when I went to the refrigerator to get some for breakfast, I found that every last bit of it had been eaten. I didn't get even another taste.

Preheat the oven to 375°F.

Scrub the potatoes, prick their skins, and bake them for about 1½ hours, or until thoroughly done. Remove the potatoes from the oven, break them open with a fork, and allow to cool enough so that you can handle them. Then scoop out the insides into a mixing bowl. Fluff with a fork, breaking up the potato up into small pieces but not mashing it too fine. If the potato seems moist, slide the mixing bowl into the warm oven for a few minutes to dry it out.

Cut the bacon into pieces and fry it until crisp in a heavy skillet. Cut up the green onions, tops and all, and drop them into the hot bacon fat. Remove from the heat at once. Stir in the sugar and vinegar and stir until the sugar dissolves. Pour the entire mixture over the baked potatoes and mix everything evenly, seasoning with a bit of salt and lots of ground black pepper.

Stuff the turkey and roast in your usual manner. If you prefer to roast the turkey unstuffed and serve the dressing on the side, bake in a covered casserole for about 1 hour, or until heated through.

Barley Stuffing

TIME: 1 HOUR
YIELD: 3–4 CUPS, ENOUGH TO
  STUFF A 9–12-POUND TURKEY

2 cups water
1 cup uncooked barley
1 tablespoon butter
1 leek, chopped (or substitute
  onion)
1 celery rib, chopped
10 mushrooms, sliced
¼–½ cup chopped pecans or
  walnuts

If you have any of this left over, put it in some soup.

Bring the water to a boil. Rinse the barley and add it to the boiling water. Reduce the heat, cover the pan, and simmer until the barley is nearly tender and the water is absorbed (45–60 minutes). The barley does not have to be cooked entirely. Remove the lid from the pan and hold barley over the heat a minute or two to dry it out some.

In a heavy skillet, melt the butter, and sauté the leek, celery, and mushrooms. Add them to the barley. Stir in the nuts. Allow to cool enough for handling, then stuff the turkey and roast it in your usual manner.

If you prefer to roast the turkey unstuffed and serve the dressing on the side, bake in a greased covered casserole for 30–40 minutes, or until heated through.

Spinach Soufflé Stuffing

TIME: 30 MINUTES
YIELD: 3–4 CUPS PUFFED, ENOUGH
   TO STUFF A 9–12-POUND TURKEY

2 tablespoons butter
3 tablespoons flour
1 cup milk
3 eggs, separated
1 cup finely chopped cooked
   spinach (fresh or frozen)
¼ cup finely chopped onion
salt to taste
¼ teaspoon dried rosemary

Spinach sounds unorthodox for stuffing turkey, but its piquant flavor complements the bland flavor of the bird perfectly.

Melt the butter in a saucepan over direct heat. Stir in the flour, and cook and stir until the flour begins to turn golden. Gradually stir in the milk, cooking and whisking to prevent lumps. When the sauce is thick, cool it and gradually mix in the beaten egg yolks.

Squeeze as much water as you can out of the spinach, and mix it into the sauce with the onion and seasonings. In a large mixing bowl, beat the egg whites until stiff but not dry. Fold the spinach mixture into the egg whites. Gently spoon the soufflé mixture into the turkey. Tie the legs together and roast according to your usual method.

Easy Smoked Turkey

TIME: 12–14 HOURS MARINATING;
  2½–3½ HOURS ROASTING;
  1 HOUR COOLING
YIELD: 6–8 SERVINGS

2 quarts water
1 bottle liquid smoke (3½ ounces)
1 small (5–7-pound) turkey

When I first tried this recipe, which was supplied by a manufacturer of liquid smoke, I honestly didn't expect to like it. That was a bad guess. We took it to a family picnic, sliced it cold, and the family ate all of it, raving all the while about how good it was. If you like smoked turkey, but have resisted the cost of those in the grocery store, this inexpensive "smoking" technique for ordinary turkey should please you.

Make a marinade by combining the water and liquid smoke in a large bowl or heavy plastic bag. Put the turkey in and refrigerate for up to 24 hours, turning the turkey once or twice to be sure all parts are exposed to the marinade. I think a marinating period of about 12 hours produces just the right mild flavor. Longer marination will strengthen the smoky taste somewhat.

Preheat the oven to 325°F.

Remove the turkey from the marinade. Dry the bird with a paper towel, rub oil all over the skin, and roast uncovered for 2½–3½ hours, depending on its size. Or use any alternate roasting method you prefer. Cool the turkey before slicing.

Amish Turkey Roast

TIME: 2 HOURS, AFTER TURKEY IS
   ROASTED
YIELD: 12–16 SERVINGS

1 medium-size (10–12-pound)
   turkey, roasted
3 bread loaves
¼ cup butter
3 large onions, chopped
3 celery ribs, chopped
poultry seasoning to taste
salt to taste
3 eggs, beaten
1 cup milk

I learned this recipe from my frugal Amish neighbors in Pennsylvania. When they are going to have a large gathering, which is almost every weekend, they roast a whole turkey, cool it, and prepare this wonderful concoction, which seems almost as expandable for feeding multitudes as the biblical loaves and fishes.

The Amish use soft white bread and omit the onion. I prefer whole wheat bread and the zip of onion.

After the roasted turkey is cool, pick all the meat from the bones and cut it into bite-size pieces. Tear the bread into small pieces. Preheat the oven to 350°F.

In a small skillet, melt the butter. Add the onion and celery and sauté until soft.

Combine the turkey, bread, onion, and celery. Season with poultry seasoning and salt. Mix in the eggs and milk. Pile the mixture into a well-greased roasting pan or flat baking pan, cover with a lid or foil, and bake for 1½–2 hours, or until the mixture is very hot and browning on top. If it seems too dry as it bakes, pour water right onto the top, recover, and continue baking.

Obviously, measurements and proportions are not too important in this recipe. To prepare smaller amounts, use leftover turkey and proportionately smaller amounts of other ingredients.

The Amish sometimes serve the Turkey Roast with gravy made by boiling the turkey carcass and neck; you can also use leftover gravy.

Turkey Wings

TIME: 1 HOUR
YIELD: 4–6 SERVINGS
CLAY POT

1 celery rib, chopped
1 onion, chopped
3 parsley sprigs
1 tablespoon fresh thyme or
    1 teaspoon dried
about 2 pounds turkey wings,
    disjointed (2 wings)
½ cup water
¼ cup butter
1 celery rib, chopped
1 onion, chopped
1 tablespoon poultry seasoning
salt to taste
3 cups coarse bread crumbs
2 cups cooked corn kernels
2 eggs

Soak the clay pot in cold water for 15 minutes. Scatter 1 chopped celery rib, 1 chopped onion, the parsley, and the thyme in the pot. Arrange the disjointed wings on top. Pour in the water.

Make the dressing by melting the butter in a skillet. Add the remaining celery and onion and sauté, stirring in the seasonings. Mix together with the bread crumbs, corn, and eggs. Spread this dressing on top of the wings, put the lid on the clay pot, and put into a *cold* oven. Set the oven temperature at 400°F. and bake for 40–60 minutes, or until the wings are tender and the dressing is browned on top. Open the clay pot with the lid away from you so escaping steam does not burn your hands.

Turkey Thigh Stew

TIME: 8–10 HOURS
YIELD: 6 SERVINGS
SLOW COOKER

2 tablespoons oil
2 tablespoons butter
2 celery ribs, sliced
2 medium-size onions, sliced
6 carrots, sliced
1 cup flour
2 teaspoons paprika
dash cayenne
3–4 pounds turkey thighs
1 cup stock
salt and pepper to taste

It amazes me how inexpensive turkey parts are, but when I try to figure out ways to cook them, I think I understand. It seems worth the effort when you consider how much food you're getting for a comparatively low price. The slow cooker is a boon for tenderizing turkey parts and playing up their good flavor.

Heat the oil and butter together in a heavy skillet. Sauté the celery, onion, and carrots in it just long enough to soften them slightly. Put them into a slow cooker.

Combine the flour, paprika, and cayenne and roll the thighs in it. Brown them in the same skillet in which you sautéed the vegetables. Place the thighs in the slow cooker. Pour off any fat that remains in the skillet and pour in the stock. Bring to a boil and stir with a wooden spoon to get all the brown bits. Pour into the slow cooker. Cover and cook on low for 8–10 hours. Taste and add salt and pepper just before serving.

To make this without a slow cooker, use a tightly covered casserole and bake in a 300°F. oven for 6–8 hours. The results won't be identical but they will be similar.

Add salt and pepper just before serving.

Foil-Baked Turkey Legs

TIME: 2 HOURS
YIELD: 1–2 SERVINGS

1 turkey leg
½ onion, chopped
½ celery rib, chopped
¼ cup sliced rutabaga
2 tablespoons water
salt and pepper to taste

Depending on the size of the legs, you can figure one leg will feed two people. The steam trapped in the foil packet does a wonderful job of tenderizing the turkey and blending in the flavors of the vegetables. If you are feeding a bunch of kids, use smaller legs and allow an individual packet for each kid. Who wouldn't love having the whole *drumstick!*

Lay the drumstick on a piece of heavy-duty aluminum foil large enough to wrap the drumstick with space left over for sealing the edges. Strew the onion, celery, and rutabaga over the leg. Add water, salt, and pepper. Seal the leg in the foil, leaving space for the steam to accumulate, and crimping the edges securely so the steam and juices all stay inside the packet. Place the package on a cookie sheet and bake at 375°F. for about 2 hours or until the turkey is very tender. No need to preheat the oven.

If you want the drumstick to appear a little more glamorous than it does in the foil wrap, arrange it on a warm serving platter and pour the vegetables and juices from the packet over it. Serve with cranberry sauce and cole slaw, and it will all taste like Thanksgiving.

Turkey Picatta

TIME: 30 MINUTES
YIELD: 6 SERVINGS

Turkey masquerades as veal well enough to substitute permanently in my kitchen. The turkey breast will be easier to slice if you do it before the meat has thawed completely. Do not buy the smallest breast you find because a lot of meat remains on the bones and can't be figured into the serving count. You won't waste it if you simmer the breastbone and pick off the cooked meat for soup.

5–6-pound turkey breast
½ cup flour
1 egg
2 tablespoons water
2 cups fine bread crumbs
2 tablespoons dried parsley
1 teaspoon dried tarragon
½ teaspoon salt
2 tablespoons butter
2 tablespoons oil

Slice the meat from the turkey breast as you would carve a cooked turkey at the table. Roll each piece in flour and pound it thin with a wooden mallet. Beat together the egg and water. In a second bowl, combine the bread crumbs, parsley, tarragon, and salt. Dip the turkey in the egg wash, then in the bread crumbs.

In a heavy skillet, heat together the butter and oil and sauté the turkey pieces on both sides, a few at a time. You may need to dump out the fat, rinse and dry the pan, and begin with new oil and butter if too many crumbs fall to the bottom of the pan and burn.

Serve the turkey in any of the ways you would serve veal similarly prepared, with lemon slices or topped with a light mushroom sauce.

Hawaiian Glazed Turkey Breast

TIME: 1½–2 HOURS
YIELD: 6 SERVINGS

4–5-pound turkey breast,
  thawed if frozen
¼ cup red wine vinegar
¼ cup catsup
¼ cup orange juice
¼ cup honey
1 tablespoon soy sauce
½ teaspoon salt
½ teaspoon dry mustard
2 teaspoons cornstarch

Good hot. Good cold.

Put the turkey breast in a roasting pan and place in a cold oven. Turn the heat to 325°F. Roast for 1½–2 hours. During the last 30 minutes of that time, brush the breast with a glaze made by combining the vinegar, catsup, orange juice, honey, soy sauce, salt, mustard, and cornstarch and simmering them together about 5 minutes. It is easiest to incorporate the dry mustard and cornstarch into the liquids by dissolving them first in a spoonful of one of the liquids.

The glaze makes enough for a larger breast if you wish. A 5–6-pound breast should be roasted for 1¾–2¼ hours; a 6–7-pound breast should be roasted for 2–2½ hours. Serve any extra glaze with the breast.

Pasta With Turkey and Mushrooms

TIME: 20 MINUTES, AFTER TURKEY
   IS COOKED
YIELD: 4 SERVINGS
GOOD USE OF LEFTOVER TURKEY

1 pound fresh mushrooms
½ teaspoon salt
¼ cup white wine or water
1 garlic clove, mashed
2 cups chopped cooked turkey
1 tablespoon cornstarch
¼ cup white wine or water
1 tablespoon butter
fresh chopped chives or green
  onions
1 pound thin spaghetti, cooked
  al dente

You could use this to get rid of leftover noodles, but it will be much better made with freshly cooked spaghetti—preferably something very, very thin like vermicelli or cappelini. Ordinarily you try to keep the juices in the mushrooms; in the following recipe you want to release the juices.

Slice the mushrooms and put them into a heavy saucepan with the salt over high heat. Shake the pan a few times so the mushrooms do not burn. As soon as you see faint signs of browning, add ¼ cup wine or water and the garlic. Bring to a boil, cover the pan tightly, and remove from the heat. Allow to stand 10 minutes. Then remove the garlic, add the turkey, and bring to a gentle simmer. Combine the cornstarch with ¼ cup wine or water. Stir into the saucepan and cook until the mixture clears. Add a little extra water or wine, if needed, to get a consistency you like. If the sauce becomes too thick, work in a few spoonfuls of water or wine. Stir in the tablespoon of butter just before serving on the spaghetti. Garnish with chopped chives or green onions.

Curried Turkey Salad

TIME: 15 MINUTES PREPARING
   AFTER TURKEY IS COOKED;
   1 HOUR CHILLING
YIELD: 6 SERVINGS
GOOD USE OF LEFTOVER TURKEY

2 cups chopped cooked turkey
1 cup chopped unpeeled apple
1 cup chopped celery
¼ cup finely chopped onion
2 tablespoons lemon juice
1–2 tablespoons curry powder
½ cup mayonnaise
salt to taste
lettuce leaves
1 cup white grapes

Combine the turkey, apple, celery, and onion in a mixing bowl. In a separate small bowl, mix together the lemon juice, curry powder, and mayonnaise. Pour this dressing over the turkey and stir to coat everything uniformly. Add salt if you wish. Chill at least 1 hour before serving. To serve, arrange on lettuce leaves and scatter the white grapes on top.

Turkey and Pasta Salad

TIME: 30 MINUTES, AFTER PASTA
   IS COOKED
YIELD: 12 SERVINGS
GOOD USE OF LEFTOVER TURKEY

A nice replacement for potato salad, it makes a lot and keeps well.

½ pound fusilli pasta
   (curly spaghetti)
1 tablespoon olive oil
1 red bell pepper, sliced in strips
1 green bell pepper, sliced in strips
1 medium-size zucchini, cubed
2 cups broccoli florets
2 tomatoes, cut into wedges
2 cups chopped cooked turkey
½ cup grated parmesan cheese
1 tablespoon chopped fresh parsley
   or 1½ teaspoons dried
½ cup olive oil or ¼ cup vegetable
   oil and ¼ cup olive oil
2 tablespoons red wine vinegar
1 garlic clove, mashed
salt and pepper to taste

Cook the pasta according to package directions and set aside to cool. In a sauté pan, heat ½ tablespoon of the olive oil and briefly sauté the peppers; set aside. Sauté the zucchini in the remaining ½ tablespoon of oil. Set aside. Blanch the broccoli in boiling water for 30 seconds and plunge into ice water to cool. Mix the pasta, vegetables, and turkey. Add the grated cheese and chopped parsley and mix well. Combine the remaining ingredients to make the dressing and pour over the turkey-pasta mixture, coating everything evenly. This salad may be served immediately, but it is better if it has a chance to stand about 30 minutes so the flavors can blend. If you refrigerate it, allow a few minutes for it to lose its chill before serving.

Simple Turkey (1 to 100)

TIME: 10 MINUTES, AFTER TURKEY
  IS COOKED
YIELD: 1 SERVING
GOOD USE OF LEFTOVER TURKEY

FOR EACH SERVING:

1 teaspoon butter
3 pieces cooked turkey
1 teaspoon fresh thyme or tarragon
or ½ teaspoon dried
1 teaspoon flour
2 tablespoons gravy or stock
2 tablespoons dry white wine or
  stock
salt to taste

In a skillet, melt the butter and add the turkey. Heat, but do not brown. Stir in the thyme or tarragon and the flour. Cook briefly to take the raw taste out of the flour. Stir in the gravy or stock and the wine or additional stock. Add salt if you wish. Cook just until hot and thickened, turning each turkey piece to coat it with the sauce. Serve hot.

Turkey Newburg

TIME: 30 MINUTES, AFTER
   POULTRY IS COOKED
YIELD: 6 SERVINGS
GOOD USE OF LEFTOVERS

4 tablespoons butter
2 cups cooked turkey or chicken
¼ cup good quality dry sherry
½ teaspoon paprika
3 egg yolks
1 cup cream
2 tablespoons chopped red
   pimento
1 cup green peas, barely cooked
salt to taste
whole grain toast, dried crisp

You can substitute chicken for the turkey in this recipe. If you do not have cooked turkey or chicken available, you can use sautéed boneless chicken breasts.

In a double boiler, melt the butter. Add the turkey and sherry and heat together for about 5 minutes. Add the paprika. Beat the egg yolks, then beat them into the cream. Gradually add these ingredients to the turkey and sherry. Cook gently over low heat. The mixture must not boil. When the sauce has thickened, stir in the pimento, the peas, and salt. For serving, rather than pouring the Newburg over toast and making it soggy, pour each serving into a shallow soup bowl and arrange the crisp toast, cut into strips or points, around the edges.

Turkey Casserole

TIME: 1 HOUR
YIELD: 6 SERVINGS
GOOD USE OF LEFTOVERS

2 eggs, beaten
¼ cup milk
2 cups mashed potatoes
¼ teaspoon baking powder
salt to taste
2 tablespoons butter
1 large onion, chopped
1 celery rib, chopped
1 cup slightly undercooked sliced
    carrots
2 cups diced cooked turkey
¼ cup grated cheese
¼ cup bread crumbs
2 tablespoons dried parsley

I started to say that kids love this, then realized that I love it. Anybody who likes mashed potatoes will love it. Because the color of the finished dish is a pale brown, it's nice to serve this turkey casserole with a bright green vegetable, such as broccoli, and sliced beets.

Preheat the oven to 350°F.

Beat the eggs and milk into the mashed potatoes, mixing until smooth. Beat in the baking powder and salt.

Melt the butter, and sauté the onion until soft but not brown. Stir in the celery, and sauté just until the celery begins to soften. Mix the onion, celery, and carrots into the mashed potatoes. Spread half the potato mixture in the bottom of a 6-cup greased baking dish. Cover with the cooked turkey. Spread the rest of the potatoes over the turkey. Sprinkle with the cheese and crumbs, and bake about 1 hour in the preheated oven, or until the top of the potatoes is nicely browned and the mixture is very hot all the way through. Sprinkle on the dried parsley just before serving.

Turkey Hash With Oysters

TIME: 30 MINUTES, AFTER TURKEY
   IS COOKED
YIELD: 6 SERVINGS
GOOD USE OF LEFTOVERS

This recipe is adapted from a very old Southern cookbook called 200 Years of Charleston Cooking. *Obviously the recipe originated in a household where neither money nor calories mattered. In fact, the original recipe suggested cooking a turkey just to make turkey hash. I find leftovers work fine.*

2 tablespoons butter
2 tablespoons flour
¾ cup stock
½ cup cream or milk
2 tablespoons butter
¼ pound fresh mushrooms, halved
2 cups cooked turkey, cut in large
   pieces
½–¾ cup fresh raw oysters,
   drained
salt to taste
nutmeg

In a saucepan, melt 2 tablespoons butter and stir the flour into it. Cook and stir over medium heat until the mixture turns dark gold. Remove from the heat and gradually stir in the stock, using a whisk to prevent lumps. Return to the heat and cook and stir until the mixture begins to thicken. Gradually stir in the cream. Do not boil once the cream has been added.

In a small skillet, melt the remaining 2 tablespoons butter, and sauté in it the mushrooms. Add the sautéed mushrooms to the cream sauce, along with the cooked turkey. When everything is very hot, add the raw oysters and continue heating without boiling just until the edges of the oysters begin to curl. Season very lightly with salt and nutmeg. Serve immediately with cooked rice and a green vegetable.

Turkey Baked With Lentils

TIME: 45 MINUTES COOKING
   LENTILS; 1¼ HOURS BAKING
YIELD: 6 SERVINGS
GOOD USE OF LEFTOVER TURKEY

1 cup lentils
2½ cups water
½ cup chopped onion
2 tablespoons brown sugar
2 tablespoons catsup
2 tablespoons molasses
½ teaspoon dry mustard
2 slices bacon, diced
1 cup chopped cooked turkey
salt to taste

Try this with people who complain about eating leftover turkey. It's good, but the turkey is scarcely identifiable.

Rinse, drain, and pick over the lentils. Put them into a saucepan with the water and onion. Bring to a boil, cover, and simmer for 45 minutes. Stir in the brown sugar, catsup, molasses, mustard, bacon, turkey, and salt. Bake, uncovered, in a 350°F. oven (no need to preheat) for 1¼ hours. Stir a few times and add extra water if the lentils seem to be getting too dry.

Serve with a little cruet of cider vinegar to pour on for extra zip.

Spaghetti Squash Baked With Turkey

TIME: 1–1½ HOURS TO BAKE
  SQUASH; 30 MINUTES TO
  COMPLETE
YIELD: 6 SERVINGS
GOOD USE OF LEFTOVER TURKEY

3 small spaghetti squash
3 cups chopped cooked turkey
2 cups chopped tomatoes, canned
  or fresh
salt to taste
oregano (dried) to taste
¼ cup grated provolone cheese

Remember how peculiar we all thought spaghetti squash was when it first appeared? And how about all we could think to do with it was pour spaghetti sauce over it? See if you don't like this lots better.

Preheat the oven to 350°F.

Cut the squash in half and scoop out the seeds. Place the halves face down in a shallow baking pan. Add water to a depth of about 1 inch and put the pan in the oven. Bake until the squash halves are thoroughly tender, usually 1–1½ hours; this varies with the size and age of the squash.

When the squash is done, scoop out the flesh in long spaghetti-like strands, keeping the shells intact. You may have to leave a little of the squash on the skins to do this. That's fine. Mix the scooped out squash with the turkey and tomatoes. Pile the filling back into the shells. Sprinkle with the salt, oregano, and cheese, and return to the oven until the squash is heated through again and the cheese has melted into it, about 30 minutes. Serve each half on a dinner plate alone, with any other dishes offered separately, to make this seem really special.

Turkey Cabbage Rolls

TIME: 1 HOUR, AFTER GRAIN IS
  COOKED AND ROLLS ARE
  STUFFED
YIELD: 6 SERVINGS
GOOD USE OF LEFTOVER TURKEY

2 cups cooked rice
4 cups finely chopped cooked
  turkey
1 large onion, chopped
¼ cup chopped fresh parsley or
  2 tablespoons dried
salt to taste
12–14 large cabbage leaves
leftover turkey gravy plus enough
  water to make 2 cups

Although the recipe calls for rice as part of the cabbage stuffing, if you feel like experimenting, you could substitute either cooked wheat berries or cooked rye berries with spectacular results. Just be careful not to overcook the grain before proceeding with the recipe.

Combine the rice, turkey, onion, and parsley. Add salt. Cook the cabbage leaves, a few at a time, in a deep pan of boiling water for about 5 minutes, or until soft enough to roll. Cool. Spoon a mound of filling onto the center of each cabbage leaf. Fold in the sides and roll the ends over the meat. Fasten with toothpicks. Place the rolls in a flat baking dish and pour the thinned gravy over the top. Cover the dish and bake in a 325°F. oven for 1 hour. If you do not have any leftover turkey gravy, substitute tomato sauce.

Cornish Hens, Ducks, and Geese

Cornish hens have become increasingly popular and hence readily available in supermarkets in recent years. They are so commonly sold frozen that one almost imagines they have never existed any other way. I have never seen a Cornish hen alive, with feathers; I have never seen one fresh and unfrozen. But I'm not complaining. Cornish hens freeze extraordinarily well, and breeders seem to have controlled their size so well you can root through an entire freezer case full of them and find their weight doesn't vary by more than an ounce or so.

Usually, Cornish hens weigh less than a pound each. They are frequently sold packaged in pairs, but some brands still sell them singly, sometimes slightly larger than the paired ones. It is traditional and elegant to allow a whole Cornish hen for each serving; but the larger ones, if split, serve two adequately.

Ducklings are often sold frozen too, though I *have* seen ducks still in their feathers. For roasting and other traditional recipes, a duckling should weigh between three and five pounds and should have been less than six months old when it was butchered. Those you find in the grocery store freezer case weigh about three to four pounds. Each bird will serve two people, though not amply because so much of the weight is fat, which cooks out during roasting.

When you buy frozen ducklings and Cornish hens you can safely rely on the standardization of their packaging and handling. Your one concern should be trying to make sure they have been properly stored at 0°F. or colder and have never been thawed or partially thawed and refrozen. If the frozen bird shows signs of frozen pinkish liquid under the wrapper or if the wrapper has a heavy coating of frost, don't buy it. Look for a store that takes better care of its frozen poultry.

If you should find a place to buy fresh, unfrozen duckling, evaluate it as you would fresh chicken or turkey, looking for firm flesh, unbruised and unbroken skin, fresh (nearly odorless) smell.

If you raise and butcher your own ducks, proceed according to the directions in the appendix for butchering poultry.

Simple Cornish Hens (1 to 100)

TIME: 1 HOUR BAKING
YIELD: 1 SERVING

FOR EACH SERVING:

1 Cornish hen
1 tablespoon butter
1 small onion, chopped
1 garlic clove, mashed
salt and pepper to taste

These are great when you don't want to make a big deal out of cooking but still want to eat something good. Put a baking potato and an apple into the oven along with the hen, and you will have an almost effortless company-quality meal.

Rinse the Cornish hen. Either discard the giblets or rinse them and put them back into the cavity of the bird.

In a small skillet, melt the butter and sauté the onion and garlic until translucent and soft. Do not brown.

Place the Cornish hen on a square of heavy-duty aluminum foil large enough to wrap the bird with space left over. Put the sautéed garlic into the cavity of the bird. Pour the butter and sautéed onion over the breast of the Cornish hen. Salt lightly and sprinkle with a generous amount of black pepper. Pull all sides of the foil up around the hen and crimp tightly, leaving room inside the foil packet for steam to accumulate. Place in the oven on a cookie sheet or flat pan, turn the heat to 375°F., and bake for 1 hour, or until the hen is nicely tender. You may roll back the foil for about 10 minutes at the end of the baking time to brown the skin, but it really is not necessary.

Serve immediately or hold the hens in the sealed foil for up to another hour with good results.

Cornish Hens Bourguignon

TIME: 1 HOUR BAKING
YIELD: 2 SERVINGS
CLAY POT

2 Cornish hens
1 tablespoon oil
1 tablespoon butter
4 carrots, chunked
2 onions, quartered
12 whole mushrooms
½ cup dry red wine
1 tablespoon chopped fresh parsley
½ teaspoon fresh thyme or
   ¼ teaspoon dried
1 tablespoon cornstarch
2 tablespoons dry red wine

Soak the clay pot in cold water for at least 15 minutes. Rinse the Cornish hens and put them in the pot. Heat the oil and butter together in a skillet, add the carrots and onions, and sauté over medium-high heat until they begin to brown slightly around the edges. Scatter them over the Cornish hens. In the same skillet, sauté the mushrooms quickly, without adding more fat, and scatter them over the hens, too. Pour ½ cup wine over the hens and sprinkle on the parsley and thyme. Cover the pot and put it into a *cold* oven. Turn the heat to 475°F. and bake for 1 hour.

When removing the hens from the clay pot, be sure to open the lid away from you so you are not burned by the escaping steam.

Pour the juices from the pot into a small pan. Combine the cornstarch with the 2 tablespoons of wine. Stir and press out any lumps. Stir into the pan juices. Cook and stir over medium heat until the mixture thickens and turns clear. Pour the sauce over the hens and vegetables just before serving.

To prepare without a clay pot, bake the hens and vegetables in a preheated 350°F. oven in a covered casserole for about 1½ hours, or until the Cornish hens are tender.

Cornish Hens With Vegetables (1 to 100)

TIME: 1 HOUR BAKING
YIELD: 1 SERVING

Only a little more complicated than the previous recipe, this one is so tasty you could serve it on Thanksgiving.

FOR EACH SERVING:

1 Cornish hen
4–6 whole fresh mushrooms
1 small carrot, sliced
1 small onion, chopped
top of 1 celery rib with leaves, chopped
1 tablespoon chopped fresh parsley or 2 teaspoons dried
1 teaspoon chopped fresh thyme or ¼ teaspoon dried
2 tablespoons sherry or stock
paprika

Rinse the Cornish hen and either discard the giblets or set them aside for another use. Wipe the mushrooms clean. Place the mushrooms and carrot in the cavity of the hen along with the onion, celery, and herbs. Pour the sherry or stock into the cavity. Place the hen on a square of heavy-duty aluminum foil large enough to wrap the bird with space left over. Lightly sprinkle the breast of the Cornish hen with paprika. Pull the edges of the foil up and seal tightly, leaving enough space in the foil packet for accumulated steam. Place the package in the oven on a cookie sheet or flat pan and turn the heat to 375°F. Bake for 1 hour or until the hen is very tender, and the carrot is cooked through. You may peel back the foil during the last 10 minutes of baking to brown the skin if you wish, but it really is not necessary.

Serve with brown rice and steamed broccoli for a memorable meal.

Cornish Hens With Lentils and Rice

TIME: 2–2½ HOURS BAKING
YIELD: 6 SERVINGS

This recipe evolved. I was reading a recipe for baked chicken and lentils, which is supposed to be a famous French bistro dish, and thought to myself that the spiciness of lentils would team up better with the stronger flavor of Cornish hens than with chicken. Then, as I was preparing to try it, I thought that adding rice to the lentils would smooth out the liquid and improve the protein value—and here's what resulted. I liked it so much I had the leftovers for breakfast.

1 cup lentils,
  rinsed and picked over
⅓ cup uncooked brown rice, rinsed
1 large garlic clove, mashed
1 medium-size onion, chopped
¼ cup chopped celery
1 carrot, thinly sliced
1 small bay leaf
2 cups water
1½ cups dry red wine
1 teaspoon dry mustard
3 Cornish hens, rinsed and split

Preheat the oven to 350°F.

Mix the lentils, rice, garlic, onion, celery, carrot, bay leaf, water, and wine in a large casserole which can be used on stove top. Dissolve the dry mustard in a spoonful of the water and wine and stir it into the casserole. On top of the stove, bring the mixture to a boil. Arrange the Cornish hens on top, cover, and bake in the preheated oven for about 1½ hours, or until the rice and lentils are tender. You may need to add extra water as it bakes. Remove the cover and bake 30–60 minutes longer, or until the Cornish hens begin to brown. Continue adding water or wine as needed to maintain the liquid level you like.

This can be served with nothing more than a spinach salad with sweet and sour dressing to turn into the kind of gourmet meal that will sustain you for hours of anything—plowing the back forty or chasing cabs in the city.

Cornish Hens With Braised Sauerkraut

TIME: 1½–2 HOURS BAKING
YIELD: 4 SERVINGS
CLAY POT

1 pound sauerkraut
2 slices bacon
2 carrots, thinly sliced
2 Cornish hens
6 juniper berries or 2 tablespoons
   gin
1 bay leaf
⅓ cup dry white wine or stock

I developed this recipe in the process of writing this book and liked it so well I have been eating it nearly once a week ever since. The inspiration for it came from Julia Child's recipe for braised sauerkraut. Even if you usually don't like sauerkraut, try this. It's not sour and it doesn't smell up the house. Do try to find fresh sauerkraut, the kind sealed in a plastic bag or glass jar and stored in the freezer case (or kept in glass jars or a crock if you make your own), rather than the canned sort which has been treated with heat. You can pick the juniper berries off a juniper bush.

Soak the clay pot in cold water for at least 15 minutes.

Rinse the sauerkraut in cold water, changing the water at least 3 times and allowing the sauerkraut to soak for a total of about 20 minutes. This removes the brine and its sour taste. Squeeze as much water out of the sauerkraut as you can.

Cut the bacon into several pieces and fry until nearly crisp in a heavy skillet. Pour off all but about 2 tablespoons of the fat and sauté the carrots in what remains until they begin to brown slightly around the edges. Stir in the sauerkraut and cook briefly so that the bacon fat, bacon pieces, carrots, and sauerkraut are well mixed. Remove from the heat and allow to cool enough for handling.

Rinse the Cornish hens. Split them in half. Discard the giblets or set them aside for another use.

Put the sauerkraut mixture into the clay pot, and arrange the Cornish hen halves on top of the sauerkraut. Scatter the juniper berries around the edges and tuck in the bay leaf. Pour the wine or stock over everything and put on the lid. Put the clay pot into a *cold* oven and turn the heat to 475°F. Bake for 1½–2 hours, or until the Cornish hens are very tender. When you open the lid, be sure to open it away from you so that you are not burned by the accumulated steam escaping.

To prepare without a clay pot, use a casserole with a tight-fitting lid, lower the oven temperature to 350°F., increase the baking time to about 3 hours, and check occasionally to see if you need to add more liquid.

Pick out the juniper berries and bay leaf before serving. As far as I am concerned, this dish cries out to be served with huge mounds of freshly mashed potatoes topped with butter.

Cornish Hens With Herbs and Pasta

TIME: 1¼ HOURS
YIELD: 6 SERVINGS
BLENDER OR FOOD PROCESSOR

¼ cup olive oil
¼ cup lemon juice
3 Cornish hens, split
½ cup melted butter
¾ cup chopped fresh parsley
1 small garlic clove
1 tablespoon fresh oregano or
  1½ teaspoons dried
1 teaspoon fresh basil or
  ½ teaspoon dried
1 teaspoon fresh shyme or
  ½ teaspoon dried
½ pound uncooked spaghetti

Preheat the oven to 350°F.

Mix together the oil and lemon juice and spread over the Cornish hens. Bake uncovered for 1 hour.

While the hens are baking, combine the butter, parsley, garlic, and herbs in the blender or food processor and process until the parsley is minced. Brush the hens with about ¼ cup of this mixture as they bake. When the hens are nicely browned and tender, bring water for cooking the spaghetti to a boil, add the spaghetti a little at a time, and cook just until tender. Drain and toss with the remaining butter mixture. Serve the Cornish hens arranged around the pasta on a hot platter.

Potted Duckling

TIME: 1¼ HOURS
YIELD: 2 SERVINGS
CLAY POT

4½–5-pound duckling
2 tart apples, peeled and sliced
1 medium-size rutabaga, diced
½ cup dry white wine
salt to taste

Here is a rich, unusual dish. It needs to be served with a contrastingly nippy salad such as spinach or endive, with a tart, rather than creamy, dressing. The clay pot cooks duckling to perfection, but you can prepare this recipe successfully in a regular casserole or Dutch oven, too, lowering the oven heat to 350°F. and increasing the cooking time by about 40 minutes.

Put the clay pot in cold water to soak for at least 15 minutes. Split the duckling in half. Pierce the skin with a fork in several places on each half. Then brown the halves on the skin side in a heavy skillet to remove some of the fat. As the fat cooks out it tends to spatter, so you may want to pour it off as it accumulates.

Fit the two duckling halves back together loosely in the clay pot and scatter the apples and rutabaga on top. Pour in the white wine. Season to taste with salt. Put the top on the clay pot and place in a *cold* oven. Turn the heat to 500°F. and bake for 1 hour.

When you open the pot to check for doneness, use the hot pads to protect your hands and be sure to open the side of the lid farthest from you; otherwise the steam which accumulates inside and rushes out the instant the lid is lifted can burn you badly.

The duckling should feel tender but still slightly firm when you pierce it with a fork. If you want it more done, simply close up the clay pot again and slide it back into the oven for a few more minutes.

Serve each duckling half covered with the cooked apple and rutabaga. Don't try to use the accumulated juice in the pot. It will be too greasy to be appealing.

Roast Duckling With Rutabaga

TIME: 1½ HOURS
YIELD: 4 SERVINGS

Recipes for duckling vie with one another for complexity. This one is very simple and very good. When you buy duckling, you get a lot of bone and fat and comparatively little meat. Although many cookbooks tell you a 5–6-pound duckling will serve 4, I think you do better to buy slightly smaller ones and allow a half duckling for each person. The French way with roast duck calls for cooking it rare; I prefer it done until none of the flesh remains pink, but still it should not be well done.

2 ducklings, about 4 pounds each
2 tablespoons soy sauce
3 large mealy potatoes
1 large rutabaga
2 tablespoons butter
½ cup milk
salt to taste

Preheat the oven to 425°F.

Rinse and dry the ducklings. If they were frozen, allow them to come near room temperature before proceeding. Use a small piece of string to tie the legs together. According to tradition, you should also pin the wings to the body, but I don't find it necessary. Prick the skin of the duck around the thighs, on the back, and at the part of the breast away from the peak. This is so fat can run out as it roasts. Place the ducks, breasts up, on a rack in a shallow roasting pan. Brush with the soy sauce.

Place the ducks in the preheated oven and roast for 15 minutes, then lower the heat to 350°F. and continue roasting for about an hour longer, occasionally spooning off the fat that accumulates in the pan and brushing once or twice more with soy sauce. Turn the ducks on the rack slightly each time you do this to ensure even browning. The ducks are done when they are a rich, deep brown all over and when the juice flowing from pricks in the thigh is no longer pinkish. If you prefer rare duckling, remove from the oven while the juices are still faintly pink.

While the ducklings are roasting, peel the potatoes and rutabaga, cut into chunks, and cover with water in a large saucepan. Bring to a lively boil and put the lid on tilted to let some of the steam escape.

Boil for 20–30 minutes, or until the potatoes and rutabaga are thoroughly tender. Drain off the water. Put the potatoes and rutabaga through a food mill or ricer along with the butter. Heat the milk and gradually whip it in with a fork or an electric mixer. Add a little salt when you add the milk. It shouldn't take much because the rutabaga provides wonderful flavor.

If you want a light gravy to serve with the rutabaga and potatoes, pour off as much fat from the roasting pan as possible, place it on a burner on top of the stove, and pour in 1 cup water. Simmer, scraping the glazes from the bottom of the pan until reduced by about a third. Salt lightly and serve in a small warmed cream pitcher. If you carve the ducklings in the kitchen, you can add their juices to the pitcher as well.

Oriental-Style Roast Duck

TIME: 1½ HOURS
YIELD: 4 SERVINGS

My favorite Chinese restaurant recently served a wonderful meal featuring what they called "Westlake Duck," in which the roast duck was boned and the meat somehow fitted back together to look almost whole again. Then stir fried vegetables in a light sauce were poured over the whole thing. It was wonderful, but took the professional Chinese cook quite a long time to prepare. This recipe is my attempt to retain the taste and general tone of that dish, while making it simple enough to cook in a home kitchen during any busy day.

2 ducklings
1 tablespoon cornstarch
¼ cup cold water
2 tablespoons vegetable oil
1 cup snow peas
1 bunch scallions or green onions,
    sliced the long way
2 carrots, julienne sliced
1 small turnip, peeled and thinly
    sliced
¾ cup stock
3 tablespoons soy sauce

Roast the ducklings according to the directions on page 92.

When the ducks are roasted and ready to serve, combine the cornstarch and water and stir until smooth. Heat the oil in a wok or large skillet until almost smoking. Throw in the snow peas and stir fry, stirring rapidly with a wooden spoon, until all are covered with the oil. Still stirring, toss in the scallions, carrots, and turnips. This part of the process should go quickly, without interruption. Continue stirring and frying about a minute longer, then add the stock and the soy sauce. As soon as the sauce is boiling, stir in the cornstarch mixture, and cook and stir just until the sauce is clear.

For spectacular serving, pour the vegetables over the whole duck. However, if you want to avoid the carving difficulties this entails, have someone carve the duck for you while you are stir frying the vegetables and have them arrange the carved meat on a warm platter. Then pour the cooked vegetables over the sliced meat. Serve *immediately.*

Roast Goose

TIME: 6¼–8 HOURS
YIELD: 7–13 SERVINGS

You are most likely to find dressed geese around holidays when some specialty meat markets make a point of getting them in; occasionally you find them in the freezer case of larger grocery stores, too. When you decide to roast a goose, you're taking on a good-sized task because geese tend to be big—they can weigh up to 50 pounds, though 12–20 pounds is more commonly what you find. The bigger the bird, the older, stronger, and tougher. Also, geese are fat, even fatter than ducks. Before you cook a goose, pull as much loose fat from its insides as you can. If you want a dressing, I think it is better to bake it separately in a casserole so you don't end up eating all the fat that otherwise would run from the bird. Allow about 1½ pounds uncooked, dressed meat per person.

1 goose (15–20 pounds)
2 tablespoons honey
2 tablespoons lemon juice
2 tablespoons soy sauce

Preheat the oven to 325°F.

Rinse and dry the goose. Tie the legs together and place on a rack in an open roasting pan. Roast in the preheated oven, allowing about 25 minutes per pound. Keep pricking the skin to let the excess fat run off and spoon out the fat regularly to keep it from smoking. Basting during the roasting is not necessary because the fat makes a goose the original self-baster.

During the last 30–40 minutes of roasting, mix together the honey, lemon juice, and soy sauce and brush on the goose to give the skin a rich, brown glaze. After removing the goose from the oven, allow to stand for about 15 minutes before carving.

Game Birds

It used to be that a family without a hunter had no hope of enjoying game birds for dinner unless they were invited to the home of hunters. These days many game birds are raised domestically, and you can buy them in supermarkets and specialty butcher shops. True, you won't find a partridge tucked in with the turkeys and Cornish hens, but you probably will find geese, quail, squabs, and, occasionally, pheasant.

Game birds have in common a distinctly "wild" or "gamey" flavor, darker, tougher meat, and less fat than such fowl as chickens and domestic turkeys.

The old-time tradition for cooking such birds included allowing them to hang after slaughter in a cool place with the innards and feathers still in place to "age." Today our tastes and what we know about food safety call for plucking and eviscerating game birds immediately and then ageing them for a day or two, cleaned, in the refrigerator. With this approach you need less marinating, fewer strong spices, and simpler preparation because there is no strong "aged" (or spoiled) flavor to counter.

Game birds can be cut up and carved exactly as other fowl.

Braised Quail (1 to 100)

TIME: 1 HOUR
YIELD: 1 SERVING

I first tasted quail in a rustic lodge on Little St. Simons Island, Georgia. The cook taught us to eat quail with our hands so we could get all the meat off the tiny bones.

Although quail used to be a delicacy available only from hunters, now these little birds are raised domestically to sell commercially and you can buy them frozen in the grocery store.

To serve quail dramatically, arrange each bird on top of a serving of brown rice and wild rice which have been cooked together.

FOR EACH SERVING:

2 tablespoons butter
2 quail
2 tablespoons dry white wine or water
salt to taste
2 tablespoons chopped celery leaves
2 tablespoons chopped fresh chives or green onion tops
lemon

Melt the butter in a heavy skillet and brown the quail lightly. Add the wine or water and salt to taste, reduce the heat to low, cover the pan tightly, and steam gently for about 30 minutes, checking occasionally to see if you need to add more liquid. At the end of 30 minutes, add the celery leaves and chives and steam for about 20 minutes more, adding liquid if necessary, until the birds' legs move easily in the sockets. Steaming time depends on the size of the quail. The meat is surprisingly chewy. Just before serving, squeeze lemon juice over the birds.

Charcoal-Broiled Quail

TIME: 8 HOURS MARINATING;
   30 MINUTES GRILLING
YIELD: 6 SERVINGS

12 quail
1 cup vegetable oil
1 cup dry red wine
1 bay leaf
1 garlic clove, mashed
¼ teaspoon dried thyme
1 small onion, chopped

Here's the makings of a very sophisticated picnic.

Split the quail in half and marinate for at least 8 hours in a marinade made by combining the oil, wine, bay leaf, garlic, thyme, and onion. Stir and turn the quail occasionally. The quail and marinade should be refrigerated during this process.

To cook, light the charcoal in the grill and allow to burn until the coals are all white. Place the quail, cavity-side down, on the grill and cook until well browned. Turn over and brown on the skin side, brushing occasionally with the marinade. If the quail are brown before getting as done as you want them, lay a piece of aluminum foil loosely across them to cook their interiors.

Serve grilled quail without forks; only fingers can do justice here.

Roast Pheasant

TIME: 1½ HOURS
YIELD: 2 SERVINGS

1 pheasant
1 small onion, sliced
1 celery rib, cut in pieces
2 slices bacon
1 cup stock or ¾ cup stock and
  ¼ cup dry white vermouth
salt to taste

Allow half a pheasant for each person. If you have anything to say about it, try to get hens in season because hen pheasants usually have more meat than males. If you have several pheasants to cook, you can roast them fitted three to a roasting pan.

Rinse the pheasant inside and out. Place the onion and celery inside the cavity and tie the legs together. Place in a roasting pan and arrange the bacon slices over the breast. Pour the stock into the roasting pan, add salt, cover, and roast in a 350°F. oven for 1 hour. Remove the lid and roast about 15 minutes longer to brown the skin. Allow the pheasant to stand about 15 minutes before serving. You can use this time to make gravy if you like it.

To make the gravy, estimate the amount of liquid in the roasting pan. For each cup of liquid, allow 1 tablespoon flour and ¼ cup cold water. Shake the flour and water together in a jar until smooth. Put the roasting pan on top of the stove over medium-high heat and bring the juices to a boil, stirring to scrape the drippings from the bottom of the pan. Gradually stir in the flour-water mixture and cook and stir until the gravy is thickened. Strain into a warm bowl.

Pheasant With Wild Rice

TIME: 1½ HOURS ROASTING;
  3 HOURS FINISHING
YIELD: 6 SERVINGS

6 slices bacon
3 pheasants
8 cups water
1 large onion, chopped
2 celery ribs, sliced in chunks
½ teaspoon salt
¼ cup flour
½ cup dry red wine
¼ cup light cream
1 cup wild rice
4 cups boiling water
¼ cup pignolia (pine nuts) or
  pecan pieces

Although you lose the glamour of the whole bird at table, I think this is by far the best way to serve pheasant.

Place the bacon slices over the breasts of the pheasants and roast according to the directions for Roast Pheasant (page 100). Allow the pheasants to cool enough to handle them easily. Remove the meat from the bones in large pieces and set aside. Break up the carcasses and put them into a stock pot. Add 8 cups water, the onion, celery, and salt. Bring to a boil, cover the pot, and simmer for about 2 hours. During the last 30 minutes or so, remove the lid and begin cooking the stock down, if it has not already evaporated, so that you have about 2 cups remaining.

Strain the stock into a saucepan and return to a simmer. Shake together the flour and red wine until the mixture is smooth. Gradually stir it into the stock. Cook and stir until the mixture is thick and smooth. Put the cream out to warm up while you prepare the wild rice.

Rinse the wild rice several times to float off any foreign matter. Gradually drop the rice into the 4 cups boiling water. Reduce the heat and continue cooking, without stirring, until the wild rice is open and tender, about 40 minutes. Turn off the heat and allow the wild rice to remain in the pan briefly to dry out.

Stir in the pine nuts. Rewarm the pheasant. Rewarm the gravy and stir in the cream.

Spread the wild rice and pine nuts on the bottom of a serving platter. Arrange the pieces of pheasant on top, and pour the gravy over all. Serve with good French bread for soaking up the gravy.

Grouse (1 to 100)

TIME: 50 MINUTES
YIELD: 1 SERVING

FOR EACH SERVING:

1 grouse
milk
1 slice lemon
1 slice bacon

Grouse is considered a "gamey" or strong-flavored bird; therefore, it is traditionally soaked in milk before cooking to mellow its flavor. Given the price of milk these days, I suggest using reconstituted dried milk.

Preheat the oven to 400°F.

Soak the grouse in the milk for about 20 minutes. Drain and dry. Put the lemon in the cavity, and lay the bacon across the breast. Lay the grouse on a piece of heavy-duty aluminum foil large enough to wrap the bird and leave extra space for folding the edges. Pull the edges together in a butcher fold and crimp tightly. Place the package on a cookie sheet and bake for 30–40 minutes, depending on the size of the bird. Then open the foil to allow the grouse to brown for about 10 minutes. Serve either in the foil or on a platter with the juice from the foil packet poured over the bird.

Roast Wild Goose

TIME: 4–5 HOURS
YIELD: 4–6 SERVINGS

1 wild goose (about 10 pounds)
4 cups Bread Stuffing (page 61)
2 tart apples, peeled and sliced
¼ cup raisins
salt to taste
10 medium-size onions
water

The goose really steams, rather than roasts, in this method. Try it for an older, tough bird. The wild goose will have less fat than a domestic one, but still will be quite fatty.

Preheat the oven to 500°F.

Rinse the goose. Remove any loose fat. After preparing the Bread Stuffing, mix in the sliced apples and the raisins and use this to stuff the goose. Tie the legs together. Salt the goose. Peel the onions and put them into a roasting pan with a lid. Bake the onions uncovered in the hot oven, shaking the pan occasionally, until the onions are very dark brown. Remove from the oven and push the onions to the sides of the pan. Place the goose in the middle of the pan. Add 2 cups water, cover the roasting pan, and return to the oven. Reduce the heat to 350°F. Bake for 4–5 hours; or until the goose is very tender. You may need to add water several times during the roasting period, but be careful not to make it so high it runs into the cavity of the goose.

This recipe can be used for any other wild birds of considerable size.

Baked Stuffed Squab

TIME: 2¼ HOURS
YIELD: 6 SERVINGS

6 slices whole wheat bread
3 large onions, chopped
1 celery rib, chopped
2 tablespoons fresh chopped
   parsley or 1 tablespoon dried
2 tablespoons red wine vinegar
½ teaspoon poultry seasoning
¼ teaspoon pepper
salt to taste
6 squabs
2 cups water

I found this old recipe in the South Carolina Cookbook *and modified it to suit today's ingredients and tastes. Stuffed squab is good served with cranberry sauce, broccoli, and baked sweet potatoes.*

Preheat the oven to 350°F.

Crumble the bread into a mixing bowl. Add the onion, celery, and parsley. Mix in the vinegar, poultry seasoning, pepper, and salt to taste.

Stuff the squabs with the mixture, and tie their legs together with a string. (This eliminates the need for trussing.)

Arrange the squabs in a baking pan and bake uncovered for about 30 minutes. When the squabs begin to brown, add water to the pan and put on the cover or seal shut with aluminum foil. Bake about 1½ hours longer, or until the birds are tender.

Serve with cooked cranberries and a lemon wedge.

Squab Baked in Foil (1 to 100)

TIME: 2 HOURS
YIELD: 1 SERVING

FOR EACH SERVING:

1 squab
½ onion, peeled but not sliced
1 tablespoon chopped fresh parsley
   or 1½ teaspoons dried
1 teaspoon chopped fresh thyme or
   ½ teaspoon dried
1 slice fresh ginger root (optional)
1 tablespoon water
salt to taste
½ bacon slice

Preheat the oven to 375°F.

Rinse the squab and the giblets if you have them. Stuff the giblets, onion, herbs, ginger, water, and salt into the cavity of the squab. Lay the bacon across the breast. Lay the squab on a piece of heavy-duty aluminum foil large enough to leave space for wrapping the bird and folding the edges. Pull the edges together in a butcher fold and crimp. Place the foil package on a cookie sheet and bake for 1½ hours. Open the foil packet and bake for about 30 minutes longer to brown the top of the squab. Serve in the foil.

Eggs

A neighbor once said to me that as long as she had eggs, milk, and flour available she could always think of something to make with them to feed her family. Almost everybody ate eggs and almost everybody liked them. Then the cholesterol scare sent too many of us to the grocery store looking for little square boxes of "egg substitutes," concocted of an assortment of artificial colors and flavorings, and resembling real eggs in no significant way at all.

Fortunately, the view on cholesterol and eggs has mellowed, especially as we cut down on the amount of animal fat we consume in red meat. We can appreciate eggs again as the wonderful food they are.

Everything I have ever read about eggs says there is no difference in taste or nutritional content between white and brown eggs. And every brown egg I have ever had has had a harder shell, brighter yolk, and (to me) fuller flavor.

If you keep chickens and have your own eggs, you've already made your choice for white or brown. If you buy eggs in the store, brown ones are often several cents a dozen more expensive than white eggs. Either color, you cook them the same.

TIPS

As those knowledgeable about nutrition will tell you, eggs are excellent food. As people who eat them will tell you, eggs are delicious food—properly handled. Like any fresh food, eggs require careful treatment to retain their best flavor, and they have their idiosyncrasies. The following tips are a few ways for enjoying the best a good, fresh egg has to offer.

- To tell if an egg is fresh, place it in a bowl of water. If the egg is fresh, the end will stick up. A bad egg will float. The closer to floating the egg seems to be doing, the older it is.

- To tell if an egg is raw or hard-boiled when you get one mixed up in the refrigerator, spin it. A raw egg wobbles; a hard-boiled egg spins smoothly.
- To make a perfect soft-boiled egg, put the egg in a pan covered with cold water and turn up the heat. When the water begins to boil, the egg is ready to eat.
- Hard-boiled eggs are easier to peel if you start with older, rather than very fresh, eggs.
- Egg whites freeze well in any small, airtight container. Yolks can also be frozen; but thawed egg yolks are successful only in recipes where they can be beaten in the blender.
- Egg whites beat up to greater volume at room temperature.
- Although volumes have been written on poaching eggs, the process is simple enough to describe in a few lines. You don't need a fancy cooker. Just fill a saucepan with water to a depth of at least 4 inches and bring to a boil. Reduce to a bare simmer. Stir in 1 teaspoon of vinegar to help firm the white. Stir the water in a clockwise direction to make a little whirlpool, crack the egg, and drop the egg gently into the swirl. (If this part goes too fast for you, break the egg into a small cup first, so that it will be ready when the water is swirling.) Remove the cooked egg from the water with a slotted spoon. Poached eggs can be refrigerated and reheated just before serving by reimmersing in hot water.

Pickled Eggs I

TIME: 15 MINUTES PREPARING;
24 HOURS MARINATING

The origins of the recipe are Pennsylvania Dutch, based on the classic one-one-one formula—one part water, one part vinegar, and one part sugar. The same formula works for making pepper cabbage and for pickling green beans. In this case, beet juice replaces the water.

hard-boiled eggs, peeled and
   cooled
1 part beet juice
1 part vinegar
1 part sugar

Pack the peeled and cooled eggs in a crock or glass jar. Boil together equal measures of beet juice, vinegar, and sugar long enough to dissolve the sugar, about 5 minutes. Pour over the eggs. It doesn't matter whether the syrup is hot or cold when you pour it over the eggs. If the syrup is hot, cool before covering and refrigerating for at least 24 hours. These eggs will keep for quite a while in the refrigerator.

Pickled Eggs II

TIME: 15 MINUTES PREPARING;
24 HOURS MARINATING

Unlike most pickled eggs, these have no sugar in the pickling mixture.

hard-boiled eggs, peeled and
   cooled
1 part beet juice
1 part cider vinegar
whole cloves
cinnamon sticks
onion slices

Pack the eggs in a crock or glass jar. Boil together equal amounts of vinegar and beet juice with the cloves and cinnamon sticks. Allow about 5 cloves and ½ stick of cinnamon for each quart of liquid. Pour over the eggs. Add about 1 slice of peeled onion for each quart after the mixture has cooled.

Refrigerate for at least 24 hours before using. These eggs will keep for quite a while in the refrigerator.

Daily Nog (1 to 100)

TIME: 5 MINUTES
YIELD: 1 SERVING

A quick breakfast or pick-up, this tastes best made with very cold milk. If you are trying to consume less dairy fat, a reduced-fat milk is fine. You probably will be disappointed in the results if you use skim milk.

FOR EACH SERVING:

1 cup milk
1 egg
½ teaspoon vanilla extract
1 tablespoon sugar
1 tablespoon powdered milk
nutmeg or cinnamon

Mix all ingredients, except the spices, in a blender or with a rotary beater or a whisk until frothy. Sprinkle with nutmeg or cinnamon just before serving. You can mix this up as much as 12 hours ahead if you keep it well refrigerated. Beat or shake again just before serving if you prepare it ahead of time.

Mayonnaise

TIME: 10 MINUTES PREPARING;
   30 MINUTES CHILLING
YIELD: 1 SCANT CUP
BLENDER OR FOOD PROCESSOR

Since the introduction of the blender and the food processor into the kitchen, making mayonnaise is so easy I wonder why we ever buy it anymore. Most recipes call for olive oil, but unless your family likes the taste, you probably will do better to use a light vegetable oil, or a mixture of olive and vegetable oils for a milder flavor.

1 egg
¼ teaspoon salt
juice of ½ lemon (2–3 tablespoons)
¾ cup oil
white pepper to taste

Put the egg, salt, and lemon juice into the mixing jar of the blender or the processing bowl of the food processor. Add 2 tablespoons of the oil. Blend or process briefly. Then, with the machine on a high speed, begin pouring in the oil in a thin, steady stream, and continue processing until the mayonnaise is thick. Season to taste with the pepper and, if you wish, some chopped fresh herbs. Refrigerate to chill for at least 30 minutes before serving.

Mom's Boiled Dressing

TIME: 10 MINUTES, PLUS
   CHILLING TIME
YIELD: 1 SCANT CUP

1½ tablespoons sugar
¼ teaspoon salt
1 tablespoon flour
3 egg yolks or 2 whole eggs
1 teaspoon dry mustard
¾ cup water
¼ cup cider vinegar
2 tablespoons butter

My sister eats this with a spoon. It makes a wonderful dressing for potato or chicken salad, either alone or mixed half-and-half with mayonnaise. I've lost the recipe twice and had to make coast-to coast telephone calls to get it from Mother in a hurry. I think the salt is necessary in this dressing.

In a saucepan, mix the sugar, salt, and flour. Beat the eggs or yolks well in a small dish and set aside. Rub the mustard into a paste with about a tablespoon of the water and combine it with the rest of the water and vinegar. Gradually beat the liquid into the flour mixture with a whisk. Bring to a boil and cook over direct heat, stirring constantly, until the mixture is thick. Remove from heat. With the whisk, beat a few spoonfuls of the hot mixture into the eggs. Then whisk the eggs into the rest of the hot mixture in the pan. Return to the heat, and cook and stir about 2 minutes more, until the eggs are thoroughly incorporated into the dressing. Remove from the heat again, beat in the butter, and set aside to cool. When the dressing has cooled to lukewarm, stir again to make sure the butter is thoroughly incorporated, and chill well before using.

Hollandaise Sauce

TIME: 10 MINUTES
YIELD: 1 CUP
BLENDER OR FOOD PROCESSOR

2 egg yolks
2 tablespoons lemon juice
¼ teaspoon dry mustard (optional)
½ cup butter, melted

I claim no originality in this recipe; it must be one of the most common recipes around for making Hollandaise. It's easy and almost indistinguishable from the kind made over a double boiler.

Put the egg yolks, lemon juice, and mustard into the blender jar or food processor bowl. Blend briefly. Make sure the melted butter is bubbling and as hot as you can get it without browning it. Turn the blender or food processor to high speed and begin pouring in the hot butter in a thin stream. Stop blending as soon as all the butter is added and the sauce has thickened. You can keep this warm by pouring it into a warm pitcher and setting it near a warm part of the stove. Direct heat could cause the sauce to split, or curdle.

Spicy Hollandaise

TIME: 15 MINUTES
YIELD: 1 CUP

½ cup butter, melted
4 egg yolks
3 tablespoons lemon juice
2 tablespoons prepared mustard
¼ cup light cream

This is not a true Hollandaise sauce because of the extra ingredients in it, but it works much the same as a sauce for vegetables or concoctions such as Eggs Benedict and Eggs Arnold.

Melt the butter in the top of a double boiler. Beat together the egg yolks, lemon juice, and mustard. With a whisk, beat the egg mixture into the melted butter and place the double boiler top over hot water. Keep the water just simmering as you beat the sauce very hard with the whisk or with a hand mixer. Beat in the cream and remove from heat. This can be served immediately or made ahead and reheated in the double boiler.

Egg and Potato Soup

If anybody has ever thought up a better soup than this one, I don't know about it. It has been a favorite of mine since I was a child, and a favorite of my children from infancy into their adult years. The combination of egg, potato, and milk produces a nutritionally complete protein, if you care about the concept of balanced proteins. We like it for breakfast and for Sunday night supper. Egg and Potato Soup is one of the few recipes in this collection that I honestly think needs salt to taste right.

Your yield can be stretched or shrunk to fit the exigencies of the moment by adding or subtracting potatoes or by adding or subtracting milk.

¼ cup butter
1 leek, white part only, chopped
1 onion, chopped
1 celery rib, leaves and all,
  chopped
6–8 potatoes, peeled and chunked
water
2 cups milk
6 hard-boiled eggs, peeled and
  diced
salt to taste
raw chopped onion
grated cheddar cheese

Melt the butter in a large soup pot. Add the leek, onion, and celery, and sauté until all are soft and golden. Add the potatoes and enough water to cover them by about 1 inch. Bring to a boil and cook, covered, until the potatoes are so tender they fall apart. Use a wooden spoon or potato masher to stir and break them into bits. The potato-water mixture will be quite thick. Stir in the chopped eggs and the milk and bring almost to a boil. Do not boil the soup again after you add the milk. Season to taste with salt. Serve garnished with raw chopped onion and grated cheese.

To serve cold, thin with extra milk and add slightly more salt.

Egg Foo Yung (1 to 100)

TIME: ABOUT 20 MINUTES
YIELD: 1 SERVING

FOR EACH SERVING:

1 tablespoon salad oil
¼ cup bean sprouts
¼ cup snow peas, cut into long slivers
¼ cup scallions, cut into 2-inch slivers
2 eggs, beaten
salt to taste
1½ teaspoons cornstarch
2 tablespoons cold water
½ cup chicken stock
1½ teaspoons soy sauce
sesame oil

This dish bears little resemblance to Egg Foo Yung served in most restaurants, where the eggs are usually cooked in much more oil. With steamed broccoli and steamed white or brown rice, Egg Foo Yung makes a wonderfully satisfying and easy meal.

Heat the salad oil in a 9-inch or 10-inch skillet until *almost* smoking. Quickly toss in the sprouts, snow peas, and scallions and stir them rapidly over high heat for about 2 minutes. They should remain crisp. Reduce the heat to medium and pour the eggs into the pan with the vegetables. Stir to mix the vegetables into the eggs. Allow the mixture to cook gently until the eggs are set. The underside should be lightly browned. If the eggs brown too rapidly, lift the pan from the heat for a moment or two and allow the heat already in the pan to finish setting the eggs. Remove the Egg Foo Yung from the pan as you would a pancake or an omelet to serve flat or folded.

If you are making the recipe to serve several people, it is better to repeat the process for each serving than to try to cook it all at once. Keep each serving warm on a heated plate as you make the others.

To make the sauce, dissolve the cornstarch in the water. Bring the broth to a boil and stir in the cornstarch mixture. Cook and stir over medium heat until the mixture has turned from cloudy to clear and has thickened. Stir in the soy sauce and a few drops of sesame oil. Serve about ½ cup sauce over each portion of Egg Foo Yung.

Eggs and Ricotta Baked With Spinach

TIME: 30 MINUTES
YIELD: 6 SERVINGS

2 pounds fresh spinach
1 teaspoon salt
6 eggs, lightly beaten
1 cup ricotta cheese
nutmeg to taste
4–6 tablespoons oil

You need fresh spinach to make this successfully.

Preheat the oven to 400°F.

Wash the spinach several times to remove all grit. Chop it finely. Mix it with the salt and allow to stand in a colander for 5–10 minutes while the excess water drips out. Mix together the eggs and cheese and season with nutmeg. Use some of the oil to grease a flat 8-inch by 8-inch baking dish. Squeeze out any remaining water from the spinach and spread it in the dish. Drizzle the oil over the top of the spinach. With the back of a large spoon, make 6 hollows or wells in the surface of the spinach and pour the cheese mixture into each one. Don't worry if some of it runs out. Bake for about 30 minutes, or until the cheese is set and the spinach cooked.

If you like a more pungent cheese, you might try this sometime with feta cheese instead of ricotta.

Eggs Arnold (1 to 100)

TIME: 10 MINUTES, AFTER SAUCE
    IS PREPARED
YIELD: 1 SERVING
GOOD USE OF LEFTOVER TURKEY

FOR EACH SERVING:

1 slice whole grain bread
1 slice cooked white turkey meat
1 egg, poached
3 tablespoons Hollandaise Sauce
    (page 112) or Spicy Hollandaise
    (page 112)
steamed asparagus or broccoli

You have to pay attention to get the name of this recipe—it's like eggs Benedict, only different. And it's too rich to be good for you, but talk about delicious . . . yes.

Toast the bread and keep it warm. Warm the turkey gently in a skillet with a tablespoon or two of water, or dip it in the water you used for poaching the egg and then drain. Place the warmed turkey meat on top of the whole grain toast and slide the egg on top of the turkey. Cover with the Hollandaise Sauce and serve with a generous amount of asparagus or broccoli to use up the sauce that runs off the egg. Have everything ready, before you begin assembling this because it's not good cold. If things get away from you, you can hold Eggs Arnold briefly in a warm oven; but if you have to do that, don't put the toast under each serving until the last minute.

Brunch Eggs

TIME: 10 MINUTES, AFTER
    POTATOES ARE BOILED
YIELD: 6 SERVINGS

2 large potatoes, boiled and peeled
½ pound bacon
½ cup chopped onion
6 eggs
2 tablespoons chili sauce (or more
    to taste)

Here's an easy way to feed a crowd. It's easily doubled.

Cube the potatoes. Cut the bacon into small pieces and fry it until crisp in a heavy skillet. Pour off as much of the fat as you can, then add the chopped onion and potatoes and cook until the onion begins to soften. Beat the eggs and pour them into the pan on top of the potatoes, onion, and bacon. Keep the heat high enough to cook the eggs without browning them, and stir gently, but almost constantly, to scramble them. Just as the eggs are nearly set, stir in the chili sauce. Serve very hot.

Zucchini-Cheese Omelet

TIME: 15 MINUTES
YIELD: 4–6 SERVINGS

1 cup sliced zucchini
2 tablespoons butter
6 eggs
2 tablespoons water
1 teaspoon chopped fresh basil or
    ½ teaspoon dried
salt to taste
⅓ cup grated smoked cheddar
    cheese

Egg brings out the flavor of zucchini beautifully. You don't have to use a smoked cheese, but if you do, you will find the flavor combination is unique.

In a 10-inch skillet, sauté the zucchini in the butter over high heat until lightly browned. Beat together the eggs, water, basil, and salt, and pour over the zucchini. Reduce the heat to medium-low, and cook without stirring until the eggs are partially set. With a spatula, lift the edges and tilt the skillet so the uncooked egg will run underneath. Before the egg has completely set, sprinkle the salt and grated cheese on top, and cover the pan until the cheese begins to melt. Fold the omelet in half and slide onto a warm plate to serve.

Mexican Omelet (1 to 100)

TIME: 5 MINUTES
YIELD: 1 SERVING

Nobody really needs a recipe for omelets, but this one seems unusual enough to write down.

FOR EACH SERVING:

2 eggs
2 tablespoons chopped canned
　　green chilies
¼ cup grated cheddar cheese
2 tablespoons sliced black olives
1 tablespoon butter
½ tomato, sliced
½ avocado (optional)
1 tablespoon sour cream

Beat together the eggs, chilies, cheese, and olives. Heat a heavy 8-inch skillet and add the butter. It should be hot enough to melt rapidly but not brown. Swirl the butter around to coat the sides and bottom of the pan and immediately pour in the eggs. Cook over medium-high heat, agitating the pan or lifting the edges of the omelet with a fork to speed cooking. Roll the omelet out of the pan onto a serving dish, or fold it in half and lift it out with a spatula. Garnish with sliced tomato, avocado slices, and sour cream. Serve at once.

Onion Pie

TIME: 45 MINUTES
YIELD: 6 SERVINGS

Serve Onion Pie for brunch or supper. I like this dish because, while not heavy, it keeps you feeling satisfied for a long time.

4 cups thinly sliced onions
¼ cup butter
1 cup coarse saltine cracker crumbs
¼ cup butter, melted
1½ cups milk
4 eggs, beaten
salt to taste
½ cup grated cheese (Swiss or
　　cheddar)

Preheat the oven to 350°F.

In a large skillet, sauté the onions in ¼ cup butter until they are soft. Do not brown. Use some of the ¼ cup melted butter to grease a 10-inch pie plate. Mix the cracker crumbs with the remaining melted butter. Press the buttered cracker crumbs against the sides and bottom of the plate. Spread the onions over the crumbs. Mix the milk and eggs; pour over the onions. Sprinkle on the salt and then the grated cheese. Bake 25–30 minutes, or until the custard is set. Serve hot or at room temperature.

Beer Cake

TIME: 1½ HOURS BAKING;
   1 HOUR COOLING
YIELD: 10-INCH CAKE
FOOD PROCESSOR

"This is the worst stuff I ever tasted," my friend said when he tried my Beer Cake. I mention him because he's the only person in ten years who hasn't liked it. I think it's wonderful.

It uses up a whole dozen eggs, keeps well in the refrigerator, freezes well, and makes a great lunch, snack, or breakfast. It contains not one bit of beer; the name comes from its origin as a traditional New Year's Eve treat.

1 pound cooked ham,
   finely chopped
1 pound bacon, diced
2 bunches green onions, chopped
1 pound brick or Swiss cheese,
   grated
2½ cups flour
1 dozen eggs
½ teaspoon salt

If you use the food processor, chop the ham and onions and grate the cheese in separate batches. You will have to cut the bacon by hand. It turns into a big lump of fat in the food processor. Put all the chopped and grated ingredients into a large mixing bowl.

Preheat the oven to 350°F.

Gradually work in the flour, stirring to coat all the little chopped pieces with flour. Beat the eggs until foamy. (You can do this in the food processor, or a blender, or by hand.) Pour the eggs into the chopped mixture gradually, stirring enough to blend thoroughly and moisten all the flour, but do not beat.

Spread the batter into a well-greased 10-inch tube pan and smooth the top lightly with a spatula. Bake for 1½ hours. Sometimes excess fat accumulates on top as the Beer Cake bakes. Pour this off if you wish.

Allow the cake to stand until cool before removing from the pan. It's good served lukewarm or chilled.

Egg Pilau

TIME: 30–40 MINUTES
YIELD: 4 SERVINGS

I never encountered anything like this until I moved to Columbia, South Carolina. It seems to me to be a kind of Southern version of spaghetti a la carbonara, using rice instead of spaghetti. The principle of letting the heat of the cooked rice cook the eggs is the same. The recipe I first saw used white rice, but brown rice makes a more tasty and nutritionally superior concoction.

1 cup uncooked brown rice
2 cups stock
salt to taste
3 eggs
2 tablespoons butter

Wash the rice if it needs it. Bring the stock to a boil, add the rice and salt, and cover the pan tightly. Reduce to a simmer and cook until the rice is tender and the liquid absorbed.

Beat the eggs in a small bowl. When the rice is cooked, stir in the butter and then the eggs. The heat of the rice will cook the eggs and melt the butter. If you are serving this for breakfast, tomatoes or canned pineapple slices would make a nice garnish; at supper or lunch time, try watercress.

Country Soup (1 to 100)

TIME: 10 MINUTES, AFTER SOUP IS PREPARED
YIELD: 1 SERVING

This is tremendously satisfying on a cold night or when you're feeling out-of-sorts.

FOR EACH SERVING:

1 cup Chicken Gumbo Soup (page 16)
1 slice whole grain bread, dried and toasted crisp
1 poached egg
1 tablespoon grated parmesan cheese

While you are drying and toasting the bread, heat the Chicken Gumbo Soup. Poach the egg. Pour the soup into a warm bowl, place the crisp bread on top, slide the poached egg onto the bread, and sprinkle everything with the parmesan cheese. Serve quickly, before the bread begins soaking up all the soup.

Scalloped Eggs and Tomatoes

TIME: 35–45 MINUTES
YIELD: 6–8 SERVINGS

1 quart canned tomatoes
  (1-pound can)
1 tablespoon cornstarch
1 cup bread cubes
1 large onion, sliced
2 tablespoons butter
1 tablespoon sugar
1 tablespoon chopped fresh basil
  or 1 teaspoon dried
6–8 eggs

Preheat the oven to 350°F.

Pour off a little tomato juice and blend with the cornstarch.

Pour the tomatoes into a 1½-quart or 2-quart casserole. Stir in the bread cubes and allow to stand while you sauté the onion in the butter in a large skillet. Add the sautéed onion to the tomatoes. Stir in the sugar, basil, and cornstarch. Place the casserole, uncovered, in the preheated oven, and bake until the casserole begins to bubble and the cloudiness from the cornstarch begins to clear.

At this point, add the eggs in one of two ways: Break them onto the top of the tomatoes and return to the oven until they are set, or poach them in water on top of the stove and then put them on top of the tomatoes. If you poach the eggs first, return the casserole to the oven only long enough for the tomatoes to bubble up around the eggs. I prefer the second method because the yolks always seem to get too hard when I try to cook the eggs in the oven. But the oven way is the traditional way. Serve very hot.

Egg Bread

TIME: ABOUT 3 HOURS
YIELD: 4 LOAVES

2 packages active dry yeast
2½ cups warm water
6 tablespoons honey
2 teaspoons salt
⅓ cup vegetable oil
4 eggs, beaten
about 8⅔ cups unbleached
   all-purpose flour

Easier to make than most yeast breads, this one is also better. It's flavorful and delicate and makes scrumptious toast. I've been making it for 15 years.

Dissolve the yeast in the warm water with the honey. Allow to stand in a warm place until the mixture is frothy, about 15 minutes. Add the salt, oil, and beaten eggs. Gradually stir in the flour until you have a stiff dough tending to pull away from the sides of the bowl. Dump the dough onto a floured surface; wash and grease the bowl. Knead the dough very lightly, probably not more than 3 or 4 minutes, to be sure it is thoroughly mixed. It will still be sticky. Do not overknead or the bread will be tough. Put the dough back into the bowl, grease the top, and cover with a towel. Allow to stand in a warm place for about 1½ hours, or until triple in bulk.

Gently knead down the dough and shape into four loaves. You may braid them if you like the look of challah. Fit the loaves into any greased baking pans that the dough will fill by about half. Exact size is not important. If you have two small pans and one larger one, adjust the sizes of the loaves accordingly and bake three loaves instead of four. Just remember to bake the larger one longer. Allow the loaves to stand in a warm place until they have risen to about double in bulk. Meanwhile, preheat the oven to 375°F. Bake for about 25–30 minutes, or until the bread pulls away from the sides of the pan and sounds hollow when you tap it on the bottom.

This bread is better cool than hot.

Miss Willie's Sweet Potato Pie

TIME: 1–1¼ HOURS
YIELD: 2 PIES
FOOD PROCESSOR

Miss Willie is a tiny lady, well into her 80s, who works in my husband's office. Not only does she refuse to retire, she works when she goes home—baking pies and other Southern wonders for the people in the office. When she found out that I had never had sweet potato pie, she sent one to me, along with the recipe and some extra pie dough so I could make my own. I think it's much better than pumpkin pie. And if you reduce the amount of sugar you use, sweet potato pie makes a good lunch dish rather than a dessert. Miss Willie would never do such a thing, but sometimes I add a splash of Cointreau to pique the flavor of the sweet potatoes. When you make this, use yams, the bright orange tubers, not the pale yellow ones we usually call sweet potatoes.

4 medium-size sweet potatoes
½ cup butter, melted
8-ounce can evaporated milk
4 eggs
½–1 cup sugar
2 tablespoons lemon juice
2 unbaked 9-inch or 10-inch pie
   shells
nutmeg or cinnamon

Preheat the oven to 350°F.

Boil the sweet potatoes until their skins burst, about 20–30 minutes, or bake at 350°F. for 1 hour. Cool just enough to handle, and scoop out the flesh into the bowl of the food processor or into a large mixing bowl. Add the butter, milk, eggs, sugar, and lemon juice. Process or beat until smooth. Pour into the unbaked pie shells, stopping about ½ inch from the top. Sprinkle on nutmeg or cinnamon. If you have extra filling left, bake it in a custard cup set in water. Bake the pies for 25–40 minutes, or until the filling is just set all the way through and the crust is evenly brown. Cool before serving.

Pumpkin Mousse

TIME: 30 MINUTES PREPARING;
  3 HOURS CHILLING
YIELD: 6 SERVINGS

1 envelope unflavored gelatin
¼ cup orange juice
5 eggs, separated
½ cup sugar
1 tablespoon grated orange rind
1 cup canned pumpkin (cooked
  puree)
½ teaspoon ground cinnamon
½ teaspoon ground nutmeg
¼ cup sugar
1 cup whipping cream

You might try this chilled pumpkin dessert some holiday in place of the traditional pumpkin pie. It sounds complicated but actually is not.

In the top of a double boiler, mix the gelatin and orange juice and allow to stand until softened. Meanwhile, in a small bowl, beat the egg yolks, then beat in the ½ cup sugar and the orange rind. Stir into the gelatin. Place the top of the double boiler *over*, not *in*, gently simmering water. Cook, stirring constantly, until the gelatin dissolves and the mixture thickens slightly. Remove from the heat and chill until the mixture is partly set.

In a separate bowl, mix the pumpkin and spices. Stir this into the chilled gelatin mixture.

Beat the egg whites until they form soft peaks, then beat in the ¼ cup sugar gradually, beating until the peaks are stiff. Fold the egg whites into the pumpkin mixture. Whip the cream until stiff. Fold it into the mixture, too. Spoon into a buttered 1½-quart mold. Cover and chill. To serve you may unmold the mousse by dipping the mold briefly into a pan of hot water, or you can avoid that tension by, spooning the mousse into dessert dishes.

Cream Puffs

TIME: 1¼ HOURS
YIELD: ABOUT 24 MEDIUM-SIZE
   PUFFS

1 cup white flour, sifted and then
   measured
½ cup butter
1 cup boiling water
4 eggs
filling (page 127)

Cream puffs were one of my mother's answers to the problem of too many eggs back in the days when we kept a hundred or so chickens (and shelled all the corn they ate by hand). The puffs used up 4 eggs and their filling used at least 8 more. This is the recipe she uses. I think it is fairly common, but it works so well I hesitate to tamper with it trying to be original. Don't substitute margarine for the butter; recipes often suggest that, but it doesn't work well.

Preheat the oven to 400°F.

After sifting and measuring the flour, sift it again. In a saucepan, combine the butter and boiling water and cook over low heat until the butter melts. Dump in all the flour at once and, keeping the pan over the heat, stir hard with a wooden spoon until the mixture forms a ball that follows the spoon around and comes clean from the sides of the pan. Do not shortcut this step because the puffs won't puff properly if you do. Finally, remove from heat, beat in the eggs, one at a time, beating very hard after each addition.

When you have a thick dough, drop the mixture by the tablespoon onto a greased baking sheet, leaving at least 2 inches between each puff. Bake in the preheated oven for 35–40 minutes, or until puffed and brown. The sides and top should be quite crispy. Remove from the oven, place on a rack, and immediately make a small hole or slit in each puff to release steam. Remove any damp batter you find inside. Cool thoroughly before filling.

Rich Cheesecake

TIME: 1½ HOURS BAKING; 1 HOUR
   COOLING
YIELD: 12 SERVINGS
FOOD PROCESSOR

Calling this cheesecake rich is an understatement. I first tasted it in an Italian restaurant. I hounded the proprietor until he wrote out the recipe for me on the back of a napkin. He said it had been his family's time-honored recipe but that he had simplified it so that anybody could make it. Obviously, any recipe calling for 3 pounds of cream cheese and half a dozen eggs makes a very large cheesecake. Plan it for a holiday meal when you expect lots of guests. A nice feature is the absence of the boring crumb crust.

3 pounds cream cheese
1 cup sugar
1 cup plus 2 tablespoons cream
¾ cup water
1 tablespoon cornstarch
6 eggs
1 tablespoon vanilla or lemon
  extract (or a combination of
  both)

Preheat the oven to 325°F.

Have all ingredients at room temperature. Beat the cream cheese to a paste in the food processor (or with an electric mixer in a large bowl). Beat in the sugar and cream and continue beating until the sugar is dissolved. Combine the water and cornstarch and blend until smooth. Gradually add the cornstarch mixture, eggs, and flavoring. When everything is thoroughly mixed, pour into a large 10–12-cup casserole. The batter will not fill the dish, but the cheesecake puffs considerably while baking. I use an iron casserole covered in enamel and lined with teflon with excellent results. Set the baking dish in a larger pan filled with hot water and bake in the preheated oven for about 1½ hours.

To test for doneness, insert a knife near the center. It should come out *almost* clean. Remove the cheesecake from the oven while slightly underdone because it will continue to cook and set up inside as it cools. It should be fairly soft and light, not hard and dry when you serve it.

This cheesecake cannot be unmolded from the pan. Cut it in slim wedges and lift each piece out with a spatula.

Vanilla Pudding (Cream Puff Filling)

TIME: 45 MINUTES
YIELD: 4½ CUPS (ENOUGH FOR 12–
   15 PUFFS)

4 tablespoons cornstarch
1 cup sugar
4 cups milk, scalded
8 egg yolks
2 teaspoons vanilla extract

You can find hundreds of elaborate fillings for cream puffs and cakes; but for me, this old-fashioned, simple recipe is the most satisfying.

In the top of a double boiler, mix the cornstarch and sugar and gradually beat in the hot milk. Beat the egg yolks in a small bowl, beat in some of the hot milk mixture, and gradually beat the egg mixture into the rest of the milk in the top of the double boiler. Place the top of the double boiler *over*, not *in*, simmering water. Cook and stir constantly until the pudding is thick. You can do this over low direct heat rather than in a double boiler, if you are careful to keep stirring the mixture off the bottom of the pan. Cool the cooked pudding and stir in the vanilla. Chill before serving.

Breakfast Cheesecake

TIME: 1½ HOURS BAKING; 1 HOUR
    STANDING; 1 HOUR COOLING
YIELD: 9-INCH CAKE
FOOD PROCESSOR

2 pounds cottage cheese
¼ cup melted butter
4 eggs
½ cup sugar
½ cup flour
2 tablespoons lemon juice
½ teaspoon vanilla extract

Think of this as my apology for the previous rich wickedness. It is neither too rich nor too sweet and packs enough protein to make a wonderful breakfast served with fresh fruit. Again, I offer it without the ubiquitous crumb crust. You can add one, if you like, by pressing buttered graham cracker crumbs around the sides and bottom of a springform pan.

Preheat the oven to 300°F.

Press the cottage cheese through a fine sieve. You may skip this step if you are using a food processor. In the bowl of the processor or in a large mixing bowl, mix together the cottage cheese, butter, eggs, sugar, flour, lemon juice, and vanilla. Beat or process until the mixture is very smooth. Pour into a 9-inch springform pan or 6–8-cup casserole (you don't need a springform pan as long as you are willing to cut out each serving individually) and bake in the preheated oven for 1½ hours, or until the cake is just firm in the center. Turn off the heat and allow the cake to stand in the oven 1 hour more. Then cool to room temperature.

Served with fresh pineapple or with orange slices, this makes a breakfast or lunch that will keep you going for hours.

Angel Food Cake

TIME: 30 MINUTES PREPARING;
   45 MINUTES BAKING; 2 HOURS
    COOLING
YIELD: 9-INCH CAKE

1 cup cake flour
1¼ cups sugar
½ teaspoon salt
1¼ cups egg whites (10–12 whites)
2 tablespoons water
1 teaspoon cream of tartar
½ teaspoon almond extract

If the only angel food cake you've ever had came out of a box, you've never had angel food cake. Long before anybody had thought to put cakes in boxes and charge you extra for adding the expensive ingredients yourself, my mother was making angel cakes for every special occasion from birthdays to Christmas. A "scratch" angel cake may not rise quite as high as one from a mix, though often it will, depending on the freshness of the egg whites, but its texture is tender rather than rubbery, and its flavor is delicate beyond description. It's not hard to make angel cake from scratch, but I think you really do need an electric mixer to beat the egg whites. This recipe is classic.

Preheat the oven to 350°F.

Sift the flour twice before measuring it; sift the sugar twice before measuring it. Sift the flour, mixed with ½ cup of the sugar and the salt, 3 times more. Have the egg whites at room temperature. Whip them until frothy, adding in the water as you beat. Next whip in the cream of tartar (this helps the whites hold up) and continue whipping until the whites are stiff and form firm peaks, but are not dry. Gradually whip in the remaining sugar, a tablespoon at a time. With a rubber spatula, fold in the almond extract. Sift the flour-sugar mixture over the beaten whites, about ¼ cupful at a time, lightly folding it in each time with a spatula. Pour the batter into an *ungreased* 9-inch tube pan and bake for about 45 minutes, or until the surface of the cake is brown and firm and the space in the cracks is dry. Invert the pan on a funnel or bottle stuck through the tube to cool. Do not remove the cake from the pan for about 2 hours, or until thoroughly cool. You can frost angel cake if you want to, but I think it would be a shame to spoil its natural delicacy with unnecessary gilding.

Appendixes

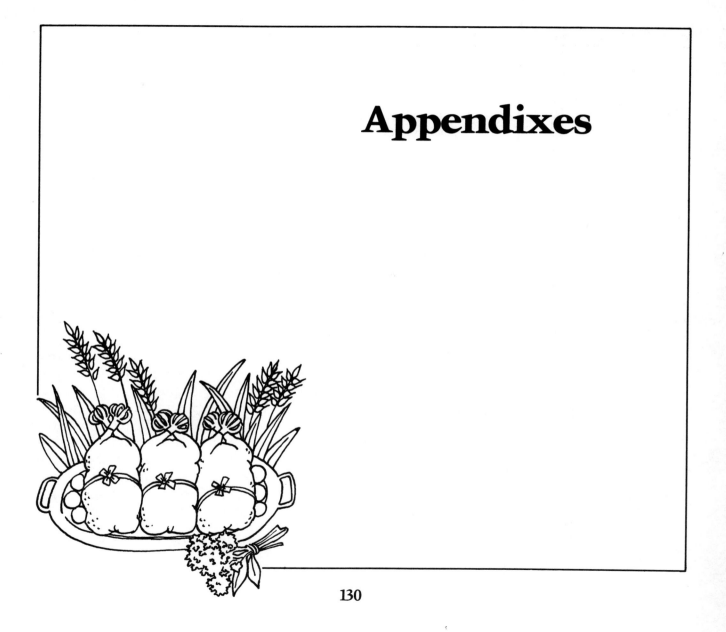

BUTCHERING POULTRY

Although butchering and dressing chickens, ducks, and turkeys probably isn't something most of us would choose to do for fun, a number of genuine advantages inhere in doing it yourself. For one thing, the poultry you raise and dress yourself tastes better. You control its feed and the rate of its weight gain so that you can allow time for the good flavors to develop during the natural maturation of the bird. Nutritionally, you avoid unnecessary fat, growth hormones, and the unknowns of commercial cage raising. Also important, when you raise and slaughter your own poultry, you are completely involved in the entire cycle by which we feed ourselves; you know chicken doesn't drop from heaven in little rectangular styrofoam trays wrapped in plastic. You take responsibility for your own part in the natural food cycle. The following instructions will help you handle poultry butchering simply and matter-of-factly.

First, confine poultry to be killed for twenty-four hours before butchering; withhold food, but provide water.

To slaughter, the old-fashioned method was to cut off the bird's head with a hatchet, or to wring its neck and then cut off the head; but a less frenetic way is to hold the bird upside down by the feet for a minute; this may lull the bird somewhat. Then you can slide the head and neck of the bird into a cone suspended from hooks, and cut its throat by inserting the knife into the neck close to the neckbone, turning the knife outward and severing the jugular. Or pierce through the roof of the mouth into the brain with an ice pick or sharp knife. These cones are available at farm supply stores, or you can make one by cutting down a plastic bottle.

However you have killed the bird, restrain the head until the bleeding and flopping stops. Leave the body hanging to bleed out for

Slide the neck and head of the bird into the cone.

Pierce through the roof of the mouth into the brain with an ice pick or a sharp knife.

Dip the bird into scalding water.

Pluck the bird beginning with the wings and tail.

Remove the remaining feathers and hair by singeing.

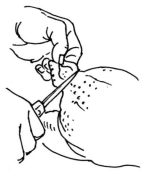

Remove the tail and the oil sack above it.

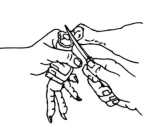

Cut off the feet.

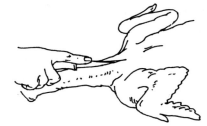

Slit the skin the length of the neck down the back.

Pull out the crop and windpipe from the neck cavity.

132   THE MORE THAN CHICKEN COOKBOOK

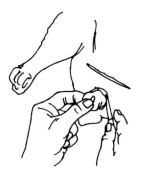

Cut carefully around the vent. Make horizontal cut above the vent.

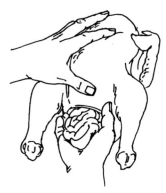

Pull gently to remove viscera.

about half an hour. When the bleeding stops, dip the bird in scalding water (160–180°F.) for 30–60 seconds to loosen the feathers. To pluck the bird, spread newspapers or brown paper on a table, lay the bird on it, and pull out the feathers, beginning with the wings and tail. After the larger feathers are plucked, you may want to go over the bird with a knife to scrape off smaller ones you missed. Any remaining tiny feathers and hairs may be removed by singeing, that is by rotating the bird over an open flame to burn off the feathers and hairs.

After you have the outside of the bird properly cleaned, it must be eviscerated. To do this, turn the bird on its back and make a wedge-shaped cut above the tail to remove the tail and the oil sac above it. Cut off the feet. (Save them and scald them to use for soup stock, if you like.) Cut off the head and slit the skin the length of the neck down the back, or more simply, just cut off the neck. Pull out the crop and windpipe from the neck cavity. The idea behind trying to save all the neck skin is to leave a flap to fold over if you want to stuff the neck cavity.

Cut around the vent to open it wider, but be careful not to cut into the intestine. Make another cut, horizontally, about 1½–2 inches below the vent. Reach through this with your fingers to work the intestines loose and gently pull them from the body. Reach through the front (neck) opening to remove the lungs, liver, heart, and gonads.

This all sounds quite complicated, but when you actually are doing it, it's simply a matter of getting hold of everything inside the bird and gently pulling it loose and out, through whichever end seems closest. If the bird was a hen, you may find the yolks of unlaid eggs inside. I'm sure that in hard times it would be wise to set these aside in a cool place to cook later; I've always discarded them with the entrails. You will know you are done with this eviscerating step when you look inside the bird and see nothing but flesh and bones.

Hang the bird to drain away all the water.

Now wash under a strong stream of cold water to remove any loose particles that may have stuck inside, then wash the outside, too, and hang the bird to drain away all the water. As soon as the bird has drained (about 20 minutes), refrigerate it until it is thoroughly chilled before proceeding with cooking or freezing. It is especially important to note that you must *never* try to freeze poultry until it is thoroughly chilled. I learned the hard way, years ago, that if you freeze a bird too soon it smells so foul in the cooking later on that you have no temptation whatsoever to eat it, which probably has kept more than one person alive.

At this point, you may want to cut up the bird according to the directions on page 26. Follow the same directions for turkeys and ducks.

Fresh poultry may be refrigerated for two, possibly three, days before cooking. If you plan to freeze it, wrap it tightly in *freezer* paper—aluminum, plastic, or white paper coated with shiny surface—not with ordinary kitchen-weight papers. As you wrap the chilled poultry, force as much air out of the package as possible. Use the butcher's seal, pulling the ends of the paper together and then folding them down toward the poultry about ½ inch per fold. Seal with freezer tape. Ideally, the freezer into which you put the poultry for freezing should be at 0°F. or below. In reality, if you use the freezing compartment of a refrigerator, the temperature will be higher. The quality still will be acceptable. The lower temperatures are more important when it comes to keeping the frozen poultry. In your refrigerator's freezer, you should keep poultry only for about two months. In a "deep-freeze," it will keep up to six months without loss of quality, if packaged airtight.

To use frozen poultry, thaw it on a refrigerator shelf for about half a day, or about 3 hours per pound. If you are in a hurry, put the wrapped package under cold running water. Microwave ovens nearly all come with instruction for thawing frozen meats and poultry. The method seems inferior to me, but in an emergency I suppose it would be worth trying.

Whether you use your poultry fresh or freeze it first, treat it just as you would purchased poultry in preparing the recipes in this book. The one difference is that the poultry you raised and butchered yourself is almost certain to be of higher quality and taste better than what you would buy.

DRESSING GAME BIRDS

We've come a long way in our ideas of how to treat game birds. I've read some descriptions of how to leave them hanging, feathers and intestines intact, that make me wonder how anybody who ate them survived. Essentially, treat game birds as you would any other poultry. Presumably it is already dead when you come in contact with it and so killing it will not be a problem.

Game birds should be eviscerated as soon as possible, and they are easier to pluck while they are still warm. This may mean doing the job in the field. If you bring your prey home to clean, you probably will have to resort to the scalding water dip to loosen the feathers.

Although some cookbooks still advise against washing game birds after cleaning, I feel it is much better to wash them. I have never noticed any loss of quality as a result of a good rinse under running cold water.

As for cutting up and freezing, just realize that structurally all game birds are put together about like a chicken—some are bigger, some smaller—but you will find the same joints and cutting places in the same places. Game birds usually have less fat in the flesh than domestic ones, so you may find they store less well in the freezer.

INDEX